Of hogs and cats

My animal diary 2021

Bibliographische Information der Deutschen Nationalbibliothek: Die
Deutsche Nationalbibliothek verzeichnet diese Publikation in der Deutschen
Nationalbibliographie; detaillierte bibliographische Daten sind im Internet
über dnb.dnb.de abrufbar.
© 2022 Bali Kiknadze
Herstellung und Verlag: BoD – Books on Demand, Norderstedt
ISBN: 978-3-7557-9626-8

*The fate of animals is of greater
importance to me than the fear
of appearing ridiculous.
It is indissolubly connected with
the fate of men.
(Émile Zola)*

*Don't breed and buy
while shelter pets die.
(unknown)*

*Only beautiful animals or
ugly people wear fur.
(unknown)*

*You can't beat anything into
the animals, but you can stroke
some things out of them.
(Astrid Lindgren)*

Preface or "what happened so far"

My name is Bali.

I started animal shelter work in 2010, after having moved from Hamburg to Berlin. My first experience was a cat sanctuary, where I fed the animals and cleaned their enclosures. When moving to the federal state of Schleswig-Holstein (that is the very North of Northern Germany), I decided to continue the voluntary work and found the cat shelter, which Bianca was running. At first, I wasn´t doing much, but as time passed by, I took over more tasks and ended up becoming the deputy of the shelter. Bianca and I have been a very good team ever since, due to our different skills.

For the shelter, I do the financial stuff, check on adopters (home visits and follow-ups), raise awareness and money, sometimes nurse kittens and help Bianca with difficult decisions.

In 2017, I decided to write a book about animal rescue (and rescuers) and did a two-year-research visiting organisations and shelters, doing interviews and taking photos. Unfortunately, the book "Paw Angels" is only available in German ("Pfotenengel", published 2019).

Since I wrote a chapter on hedgehogs in that very book, I wanted to learn more about these interesting mammals and met Ursel by chance. She handed me my first hedgehog to care for, Benjamin. He was easy: Treatment had been finished, and I only had to feed and supervise him. After that, in 2020, I got Alfred and had to prepare him for hibernation. That´s how the whole thing took off. Now, I am running a hedgehog foster care myself.

In the same year, I decided to write a diary, in order to show people how time- and money-consuming the voluntary work can be. I left out private life, most of the jobs and still: It sometimes looks like a full-time-job. And other rescue stations have even more animals in need than I do. I often wonder how they survive without collapsing.

One year of writing an animal diary is enough, I thought. However, I felt sorry, that only German speaking people will be able to read it. After all, rescuers with similar thoughts, emotions and problems can be found everywhere on our planet. So I did it again – with the hope that a lot of people will read and like it.

Yours truly,
Bali.

P.S. You will find some snapshots at the end of the book.

P.P.S. There will be grammatical errors or spelling mistakes, though I read the text ten zillion times. Bear in mind, that I am not a native speaker and didn´t want the text to be checked by a professional, since that would raise the cost of this book enormously. Besides, if you understood most things so far, you will have no problems reading the rest of the book. ;-)

Let me introduce the main characters:

Ursel
A 82-year-old hedgehog expert. More than 45 years of experience. Runs a hedgehog foster station. She is very famous in the German hedgehog scene. I am lucky to be her apprentice. We started working together in 2019. Over the time, Ursel became a lot more than my hedgehog teacher. Since I have never really had a Mum (mine died when I was five years old), I have declared her my "second Mum", which fits perfectly, age-wise. And personality-wise and heart-wise anyway, if you know what I mean. And she, being childless, is more than fine with that!

The hedgehog emergency network
That´s a network with a phone number you can call within Germany, to get immediate assistance when you find a hedgehog and don´t know what to do. Behind that number, there are several hog-experienced people from everywhere within our country. It works with a phone-app that registers the number of the caller, and whoever is available, will call back. And, as you might have already guessed, I am one of them.

Bianca
The head of our cat shelter, where I am second-in-command. Bianca is a vet tech, working for my favorite vet, and she is a true workaholic. She started our cat rescue, that mainly deals with orphaned kittens, in 2012. I am with the shelter since 2013. We bottlefeed, spay/neuter, find adopters, help other rescues and do educational work.

Bianca is always on duty, never sleeps enough and does everything she can for the shelter. Plus, she never complains. A truly fascinating and adorable lady!
And if Ursel is somehow my Mum, then Bianca has – without a doubt – the role of an older sister.

Andreas von Baudissin ("Andi")
My superskilled graphic designer. We have done two games together so far: *The temper of Titus* ("Katerstimmung", a dice game) and *A game of spines* ("Stachelritter", a familiy board game). I had the ideas and worked out the concepts, he drew the pictures. Andy is not only skilled - he is terrific to work with. So, that won´t be the end of our work relationship. I assure you, plenty of new ideas already jump up and down in my brain!

2021

January 1, Friday
Used the day off to work on the corrections for the Animal Diary 2020 (original title: *Tagebuch eines Tierschützers*). In the afternoon, I had Ursel here for tea and cake. Same thing we did last year: Starting the new year together. We were talking about Noel, a hedgehog still being in my house and on medication. When his treatment is over, he can go into "supervised hibernation". That means, he will sleep in an enclosure on my secured patio, be checked daily and after his long sleep, will be checked and treated for parasites again, before he will be released.

January 2, Saturday
Ursel was here to pick up Noel. He will stay with her until I am back from my short trip (a family funeral in East Germany). Noel had 604 grams today and received his last medicine for lungworms.
In the evening: More work on my book. I need to finish this soon.

January 4, Monday
Ramses is not happy. He is one of my two Bulgarian tomcats and extremely sensitive. He gets mobbed by Piccolo, whom I took over last November. And Pepe, the youngest in my cat group, is not much better!

He used to hang out with Monk (that's the other Bulgarian), but has now started to imitate Piccolo, by chasing Ramses around the house.

With Titus (namegiver of the dice game I had invented) dying last October, the whole constellation in my cat household changed. Titus had been the boss and Ramses was protected. Without Titus, he is an easy target, and I have to think of a way to stop that.

January 5, Tuesday

Working with my graphic designer Andi on *A game of spines*. That's my hedgehog game, that I will launch this year. Hopefully in spring. We worked on the corrections of the game rules and the event cards. I have been reading this stuff so many times that I start loathing it. Same goes for my books: Proofreading is awful. You can read the text for the umpteenth time and still find mistakes. How's that possible, for crying out loud!

Saw this morning that Mozart had been awake last night. He is one of the hedgehogs that are already hibernating in separate enclosures on my patio. The other one is Kandis, but she has been asleep since December. Her enclosure is tidy as hell. Plus, the dry food is untouched. Well, Mozart must have had a party last night. All the newspaper was upside down, and the bowls with food and water were empty. Hedgehogs do wake up every so often and these days, we have night temperatures around two to five degrees.

January 6, Wednesday

A quick drop-in at Ursel's for some tea and cake and checking on Noel, before I leave. He is doing fine.

January 10, Sunday
Went over to Ursel to pick up Noel. He looked good. But Ramses didn´t. He was lying in his cat bed the whole day, and I didn't see him eating. And what is more, he never came over to me for some intense snuggling. Now that is really weird! What the hell is wrong with him?
Also checked on Mozart and Kandis: They had slept soundly the last days. Their enclosures were neat and shiny.

January 11, Monday
Took Ramses to the vet. Oho, high fever! He got some injections. Later in the evening, he started eating again. So far, so good.

January 12, Tuesday
Ramses seems a lot better. He is running around the house and also comes up for some cozy moments into my study. Phew!
Moved Noel and his enclosure onto my patio. Let´s hope that he will fall asleep soon. It´s about time for him. His domicile is right between Kandis and Mozart.

January 13, Wednesday
Checking on my hoggies, I saw that Noel had been awake last night, which is not surprising, since hedgehogs do not fall asleep immediately. Besides, he will have to make his nest first, now that the outdoor temperature tells him to do just that. He messed with the newspaper and kicked over his water bowl. Oh, well.

Took Ramses to the vet again. He got another round of antibiotics and that should be it. We will see.

January 14, Thursday
Noel is still eating the whole bowl of food. Seems, he is not thinking of hibernation too soon.
My aunt died today. Therefore, I am glad that Ramses is sleeping (and snoring) right beside my head. He is my soulmate and gives me peace, when my own world is unbalanced.

January 17, Sunday
Ramses had been very quiet since last evening. And this morning the same picture. Piccolo chases and scares him whenever he finds an opportunity. I need a solution soon; Ramses is really stressed, that is obvious.
Was at Ursel´s for tea and cake and our hedgehog talk. These days, there is not much to do for us, concerning the hoggies. Most of them sleep. And those, that don´t sleep, are preparing for hibernation. Treatment times are over. For now, anyway.

January 19, Tuesday
Somehow last night´s heavy rain got into Noel´s enclosure. Holy shit. At least his sleeping box was dry. Nevertheless, I cleaned up and relocated his enclosure to a drier spot. Let´s see if that does the trick. The roof on my patio obviously has a leak somewhere. Sigh.
Went to the vet with Ramses and Pepe. Pepe only got vaccinated, but Ramses got another round of antibiotics. He has lost weight, and I am very concerned about him.

In the evening, I got visitors: a couple that had shown interest in Piccolo and Pepe. Yes, I am trying to get them adopted, since, young and fit as they both are, they need more action, such as outdoor activity. With the secured back garden, my residence is rather appropriate for old or disabled cats. The couple were nice and Piccolo was cool with them. Only Pepe wouldn´t show up. He hid behind an armchair and wouldn´t come out until they were gone. Hmm, what do I make of that?

January 20, Wednesday
Went to my cat shelter today. That´s a one-hour-drive, therefore I don´t drive up every day. Bianca and I went through some financial stuff, such as invoices and the donations. Then I went over to the house where the prospective adopters lived. The house needs repair, to say the least. The guy told me, that he was still working on that. Well, obviously I wouldn´t hand my cats over to a building site, so I told him to call me whenever he is ready for the adoption. But to be honest: I am not at all sure that I want my cats to live here. Something is still bugging me. And gut feeling overrules everything!

January 21, Thursday
Slept very bad last night. I have still been contemplating this couple, that might adopt two of my shelter cats. No, I am not gonna do it. Fullstop.
Went to see Ursel and had Octavia with me. She is a hedgehog at 262 grams, that Bianca gave me yesterday. Octavia was found and brought to my favorite vet.

After the initial treatments, my vet asked me to take over. So, Ursel had a close look, but found nothing apart from some mites. We can handle that, no sweat.
Took Ramses to the vet again. He is satisfied and reckons that Ramses will have fully recovered soon. Seems that he was right: Back home, Ramses was eating again and behaving quite normal.
Octavia has gained weight and is eating well too. Good girl.

January 22, Friday
Took Octavia´s poo sample, that I had been collecting since Wednesday, to the vet. For an accurate analysis, you should collect poo over two or three days. I got the results in the evening: She has a high burden of lungworm. Okay, starting treatment right now.

January 24, Sunday
Octavia has gained weight rapidly, due to the deworming. She weighed 314 grams today!
Did some home-office work for our cat shelter, such as filling in donation receipts. Same procedure as every year in January.

January 27, Wednesday
I still have an eye on my Ramses. He is not yet eating the amount he should. And he is way too quiet.
Ursel has been here, for tea and cake. She told me that Paddle-Bianca has finally started hibernating. Paddle-Bianca is a female white hedgehog, that was both in my care and in Ursel´s, and not at all easy to treat.

Her strange nickname comes from her iffy hind legs, and last year, Ursel was very worried, whether she will ever be able to use those legs again. She was paddling more than anything! After a very laborious treatment, her legs improved considerably. But she wouldn´t hibernate for a long time, just eating and eating and eating. Ursel found that quite annoying.

January 28, Thursday
Wow! Noel must have slept deeply last night: The bowls were untouched and the enclosure was tidy. Well, with the temperature gradually dropping below zero, this might be it! Or so I hope. With hedgehogs, you never know.
Went to the vet with Ramses. He had lost weight again. I insisted on a blood sample. I want to know what is wrong with my soulmate.

January 29, Friday
Result of Ramses´ blood sample: Nothing to get excited about. Pretty normal. Hmm.
Kandis, Mozart, Noel: all asleep.

January 31, Sunday
Had a long phone call with Bianca. We were discussing the possible adoption of Piccolo and Pepe. Before we hung up, Bianca told me that her dog was dying. Probably only a few days left. My heart sank. That dog was with her for so many years and was our "cat shelter dog", taking care of all the cats and kittens that we nursed, fed and treated. This is really heartbreaking news.

February 1, Monday
Started feeding Ramses in his cat bed, since he was too scared to come down to the kitchen. Poor chap. But at least he eats while I sit next to him. Good.

February 2, Tuesday
Went over to Ursel´s, for tea and cake. Told her about Noel: It seems that he is hibernating now. Well, sort of. Ramses is a lot more active today. I still bring him his food, wherever I find him, so that he cannot clash with Piccolo or Pepe. Looks like the plan slowly comes together. However, that is only a temporary solution.

February 3, Wednesday
Today is like Christmas! Lars, an old school friend of mine, who knows about my work with hedgehogs, has built a feeding station for my carport. It is handmade and really amazing. I was so thrilled, that I ordered a three-storey winter-enclosure for the hibernation period. His son, who wants to become a carpenter, will deal with this rather complicated project. The thing is this: A person, that is not a hedgehog fosterer, would not exactly know what is important, in terms of space, dryness, ventilation. So, as the "expert" you have to do a lot of explaining. Anyway, Lars and his son rose to the challenge, and I can´t wait to see it on my patio.

February 6, Saturday
Ramses is feeling and eating better. Octavia weighed 617 grams today, but she coughs sometimes. Quite normal, after lungworm treatment. I will give her expectorants, to ease the coughing.

February 8, Monday
Had a home visit today, for one of the Bulgarian shelters. I do that sometimes, if it is in my area. The shelter wanted to re-home a cat, and I visited the prospective adopter, which was a woman of my age. She had a cat already and was looking for a second one, so that they could be playmates. The thought is absolutely reasonable, but in this case, her cat is a wild one, and I fear that the cat from Bulgaria might get stressed out. The lady was very understanding, when I tried to explain to her, what kind of cat might fit better. There were more aspects that made me uneasy, but anyway, we called it off. And I was glad that the Bulgarian shelter agreed with my concerns. Mind you, checking on adopters, whether it is before or after an adoption is not an easy job. Not at all.

February 9, Tuesday
Got a call from the lady I visited yesterday. She wanted to thank me again, for having spent so much time with her and having been so empathic. Wow. It is quite rare that somebody thanks me for having done the opposite of the expected. Chapeau to that lovely lady. I promised her to help finding an appropriate cat, if she wishes.

February 10, Wednesday
What a rollercoaster day: It started with me noticing that Piccolo was very reserved and wouldn´t eat. Jesus, now what? Then I continued proofreading the Animal Diary book, with Ramses on my knees purring and feeling good. Then I got a call from Bianca: Her dog has died today. Oh, what a bummer! I felt so sorry for her.

In the evening I started to create an instagram profile, which was difficult at first, but fun in the end. So far, I have not really dealt with this medium, but my hubby convinced me, that it could be worthwhile to have an account there. You can follow me on instagram now: bali_kiknadze. All in all, that was indeed a very strange day.

February 11, Thursday
Last corrections on the book. That´s it. Now waiting for the second print-out. Also had a long phone chat with Andi about some corrections for *A game of spines*. That should be it, too. The whole thing will be passed on to the producer now. That´s really exciting. My first big board game, holy cow! Well, holy hedgehog, in fact.
Amira and Lucas, new candidates for Pepe and Piccolo, came over for a visit and get-to-know. Now that was a completely different story to that of the people that had been here some weeks ago. What a lovely couple they were! Even Pepe was around the whole time (and we are talking about sitting and chatting for more than two hours!) and let them cuddle and play with him. Piccolo was as always: Constantly around and collecting cuddles from everybody. It was a fantastic evening, and I pray to God that this couple will be the adopters of my funny duo.
By the way: This very morning, I called the guy from the other couple, that had shown interest and asked him what the situation was. He told me that he was sorry that he never got back to me, and that the renovation was still going on and that he had never expected it to last so long.

Why did he not tell me that in the meantime? For me, not getting in touch is a sign, that there is no real interest. I was polite, but very direct. That is my nature. Mind you, we are not talking about a crate of beer, but about living beings with a soul.

February 12, Friday
Got a call from Amira and Lucas: They have fallen in love with Pepe and Piccolo and really want to adopt them. Wow! I don´t think that I can get a better home for my boys. Besides, they live in Wacken. Yes, Heavy Metal Wacken. That´s only about 35 kilometers (=22 miles) away from my home. That makes me feel even better!

February 13, Saturday
Piccolo is eating and behaving normally again. But still, I feel better getting him checked at the vet´s, especially since I want to be absolutely sure, that he is okay before handing him over to a new home. The vet couldn´t find anything wrong with him. Good.

February 14, Sunday
Made the home visit today at Amira and Lucas´ house. Nothing to complain about. Besides, they live in a quiet area, a good distance away from the Heavy Metal in-field. We made a date for next Saturday. Until then, they will purchase everything necessary: Food, scratching posts, litter boxes, the works.

February 15, Monday
Woke up to a funny gut feeling. Was thinking about Haifa.

She is a hedgehog, that had been brought to me last September by a lady around 60 kms away. Haifa wasn´t injured, only had mites and lungworm. With nursing and feeding coming to an end, the lady started wanting her back for supervised hibernation. I wasn´t feeling too good about it, but gave in. So, from October on, and after a detailed instruction, Haifa was returned and the lady was happy. But I was still full of worries, though I visited her two weeks later. All seemed well, yet again I couldn´t relax. The lady gave me either little or belated information on Haifa, and that is something, I really cannot cope with. If you are a newbie with hedgehogs, at least go by your teacher. I tried to contact the lady, but when I didn't receive an answer for two days, I spontaneously decided to pick Haifa up. The lady was surprised to see me, and I apologized for my sudden visit and asked about Haifa. She was asleep in a box, surrounded by moist leaves (though I had explained why leaves should not be used as a bedding during supervised hibernation), and her water bowl was frozen over. I apologized again, but gave any long discussion a miss. All I wanted was: Get Haifa and go home.

February 16, Tuesday
Ursel called to tell me that she got another hedgehog: Marlene, 433 grams, found in the snow. She wouldn´t eat or drink, coughs a little and has a dry nose. No obvious injuries. Ursel will get the necessary meds from her vet and start the treatment right away. Finding a hedgehog, that is not hibernating in the middle of a snowy winter is bad. Very bad.

I had an interesting phone call with one of the big rescue stations in England today. After I was told that they recommend wet cat food with gravy, I called them up, asking them why they do that. The gravy in cat food can cause diarrhoea, due to various reasons. Some have to do with the additives, that are part of the food. The station agreed, that their recommendation might cause misunderstandings, taking into account that us rescuers also deal with still inexperienced fosterers, as well as weak or ill hedgehogs, and therefore cannot permit any major mistakes.

I was glad that they didn´t take my concerns as a lecture but as that, what it was: Thinking only of the well-being of the animals.

February 19, Friday
Went over to Ursel´s today, for some tea and cake. Marlene was a tricky one, she told me. First, she lost even more weight. Then, after the first lungworm treatment, she really kicked off and has now 500 grams to proudly present. Ursel herself was in good spirits, which is always a relief to me, since she is already 82 years old, and I am constantly worried that something bad might happen to her. With or without Covid-19, that is.

Update on my hedgehogs: Noel and Octavia had been awake: Food gone, papers all messed up. Haifa in the garden shed also seems to have had a peek: Some of the cat biscuits were missing, but her enclosure was tidy. I guess it´s the temperature, that fiddles with their instincts. Even at nighttime, we are well above zero now.

Mind you, hoggies mainly react to night temperatures, so the upcoming spring might trigger some of them already. But we are still in February - easy does it!

February 20, Saturday
Well, today is the very day: Pepe and Piccolo are moving out. I was nervous as hell and so were Amira and Lucas. Piccolo went about the place like he has always lived there. Pepe hid behind the shoe shelf, so finally I picked him up and tucked him into his sleeping box, which will stay there at least for a month. Cats need things with familiar smells, when in unknown territory. That´s why I also packed another cat bed and their favorite toys. I want them to have a good start with these awesome adopters. But, knowing Pepe, I believe that will take some time. Same goes for myself. It is suddenly eerily silent in my house.

Now to the hoggies: Only Kandis and Haifa were still asleep. Mozart, Noel and Octavia had been awake. Well, no wonder: with 15 sunny degrees outside! A week ago, we had heavy snow. The weather is going crazy.

Took a call from the hedgehog helpline: A lady from Lübeck found a hedgehog in her garden, secured it and wanted to know whether she should release it again or not. I told her why releasing is not a good idea, and how she could help it coming through the rest of the winter. She was very ambitious and friendly, so I will guide her until her hoggie can be released. She gave him a name too: Willy.

February 21, Sunday
Apart from the odd call over the hedgehog helpline (those calls are increasing now, due to the warm weather!), nothing much happening. Got a message from Amira: Piccolo is doing great and Pepe is also slowly thawing. She sent me a very cute photo of them. Letting go is not easy for me. Never is. Never will be.

Monk and Ramses have reacted in different ways, as I anticipated: Ramses is fine with the situation and definitely more relaxed. Monk is a little restless. Not that he cared much about Pepe and Piccolo, but he notices the change nonetheless.

February 22, Monday
Monk is howling a lot. Hmm. Until now, he was nearly invisible. We called him "stealth cat" for a reason. Is he really that much affected by the move-out of his cat mates?

Visited our local cemetery, to fill the water bowls for wild animals. I have been doing this over several years now, at different cemeteries. But I never started that early! But with the weather being dry and warm, hedgehogs, mice and other feral animals won´t be able to find any water.

Argh! Had to return home after finding out that the water had been cut off. Came back with two water bottles and filled up three clay bowls.

Ursel had asked me to get her an appointment at my favorite vet for a check-up on Lissi, her cat, that has a dodgy eye. I offered to attend to this task, since the drive is too long and stressful for Ursel. 106 km (66 miles), one way.

February 24, Wednesday
Woke up with a fantastic idea for a wildlife card game!
Started drawing some sketches immediately, before
forgetting everything and also wrote down the basic
rules.
Weather still very warm and dry, so I cycled over to
another village, that is five km away, to fill the water
bowls on their cemetery. I was smart enough to take
water with me this time!
Before I left my house, I received a message from one
of my colleagues from the hedgehog helpline: A diurnal
hoggie with a bad eye had been found, around 40 kms
away from me. I rang Ursel to hatch a plan. Ursel said
she would drive over to collect the poor thing, do the
examination and report in the evening. With all our
winter guests still semi-sleeping, we are already
running out of enclosures. Bad timing!

February 25, Thursday
Four of my five hedgehogs had been awake during the
night! I hope the weather forecast is right and
temperatures will be dropping again in a few days. This
is way too early for them to end hibernation. Update
from Ursel on yesterday´s hedgehog: It weighs 500
grams, cannot eat by itself and is slowly dying of
cyanosis. Tongue and gums bluish. The cause for a
cyanosis is a low oxygen saturation in the blood. It is
heartbreaking to think of these animals not finding
enough food and water, simply because we destroy
nature everywhere by overcleaning our gardens and
sealing the soil surface with concrete and stone. We, as
mankind, are slowly digging our own graves.

Nature can do without us. But we cannot do without nature. Why is that so hard to understand?

Worked on the wildlife card game a little more. For a break, went to our local cemetery again, to check the water bowls. The caretaker spotted me ("You here already?"), and I told him of dry soils and dying hedgehogs, and why I had to start so early this year. He is a nice man and always lets me do my work there. Besides, he offered to get water from his shed, as long as the water pipes are shut down. You see, even a little bit of support makes an animal rescuer really happy. We recharge our batteries from behaviour like his, if you get my meaning.

February 26, Friday
Checked the trail cam that I had hung up (first time this year) yesterday, high above over the hedgehog enclosures. No footage at all. Was probably too high up to catch any movement.

Had some business in Hamburg today and, on the way, stopped by at our family cemetery. Cleaned up a little (mainly leaves and twigs) and filled up some water bowls.

February 27, Saturday
Had the cam out again over night. This time on the ground and close to Octavia´s enclosure. I was extremely lucky: Octavia was the only one awake last night, but she did the full monty! I had nearly 400 files on the cam when I took it in and had a real blast reviewing the footage.

Went over to Ursel´s in the afternoon for tea and cake. The hedgehog, she collected three days ago, had died yesterday. No chance, she said, rat poison. Her foster care is almost full now. Some are still on medication, but they are all doing well.

March 2, Tuesday
A busy day lies ahead of me, but first, I retrieved the cam early in the morning: Nothing but the neighbour´s cat. That means, all my outdoor hoggies are still in hibernation. And they have a right to be: Night temperature is back around zero degrees.
At 10:30 Ursel stood in the door, handing me her cat Lissi. Ursel had gladly accepted my offer to do the long drive. The fog was awfully thick around the Autobahn, and Lissi was giving a free concert nearly all the way! At least the examination of her eye didn´t show any tumor yet, so we have gained another six months, give or take, before my vet wants to see her again. On the way back, I stopped at our cat shelter, discussed the latest news with Bianca and collected the invoices, since I do the accounting. In the meantime, the fog had lifted completely to offer a sunny day with nine degrees when I dropped Lissi back at Ursel´s and sank into the armchair. Ursel had prepared tea and cake, and we discussed Lissi´s situation as well as "Thickie"´s. Thickie is the other cat she has: He suffers from diabetes and should be injected twice a day. That proves to be quite difficult. Thickie has been an outdoor cat all his life and only comes in for food. Therefore, it's a daily game of hide and seek – some of you cat owners can relate to that, right?

March 4, Thursday
Octavia is still roaming around in her enclosure, night after night. For Christ´s sake: What prevents her from hibernating?

Got a call from a friend: Some heavy changes have taken place in her private life, and she has to give one of her cats away. Could I perhaps give him a home? Well, I said, what I really need is a cat for Ramses, who seems to suffer from loneliness, ever since my cat Nike died last October.

Seems, that the cat of my friend is a very shy one, that is mobbed by the other two and might be suitable for Ramses. We give it a shot, but no guarantee. She will have to think of a plan B, if they don´t get along here. They will come over on Saturday. Mind you, I wouldn´t do that easily, but I like this girl very much, plus, she has helped out at our cat shelter many times. I know her quite well, and Bianca, knowing her even better, encouraged me to give it a try.

March 5, Friday
Ramses is howling and throwing up. Huh?

March 6, Saturday
Got a call from the hedgehog helpline: A hedgehog was spotted around 30 kilometers away. The finders have secured it yesterday. It seems unharmed, but too skinny. Okay, I said, but they will have to bring it over.

My friend arrived with Monty, the shy cat. We sat down with him in my study for half an hour, then I closed the door, so he could cool down in there.

Back in the living room, my friend tried to be brave but couldn't stop the tears for long. I know how hard it is for her.

An hour after she left, the hedgehog was brought. Yes, very thin (278 grams), but apart from that, he seems fine. Welcome to our house, Platon.

Mind you, my hedgehogs get their names in alphabetical order. That makes the counting a lot easier.

March 7, Sunday
Ursel came over for tea and cake. And, of course, to have a look at Platon. He seems okay, she said, but nonetheless, finding a hoggie around this time with that weight always means trouble. I started collecting his poo, of course, to see what bothers him from the inside. Monty, the shy cat, is still hiding under a closet in my study.

March 8, Monday
Platon is eating well. So is Monty. I am really relieved. Plus, Monty ventured out from under the closet and let me pet him, which ended with a jump up onto my lap. Wowzers! Things are looking not too bad today.

March 9, Tuesday
Was curious how Piccolo and Pepe are doing. Got a message back from Amira, that they are doing fine, playing and running about the house, as well as enjoying cozy moments in the evening. Everyone is really happy, both cats and humans. They enclosed some pictures for me to see for myself. Yes, they look terrific. I am glad that it worked out so well for them.

March 11, Thursday
Monty is everywhere. Following me around, making high meow sounds. Funny guy. Ramses and Monk keep their cool and watch the show from a safe distance.
Platon: Keeps gaining weight. He is at 360 grams today. And he doesn´t mind the injections at all. I love him!
Did some work on the wildlife game, since it is a stormy, rainy day and I have no business outside. Talked to Andi on the phone: We will meet next week. I want to show him the concept of the game, so that he can start thinking up possible pictures.

March 15, Monday
Had a home visit this afternoon, for a Bulgarian shelter dog. The dog in question is a puppy and supposed to be the second dog in that family. They were nice, the house was cozy, their dog well-educated. I guess, I can give a green light. Mind you, there is always a remaining risk that things won´t work out, no matter how long you stay or how much you talk with possible adopters. But the thing is, that if a dog comes from a shelter within the country, it is comparatively easy to return it, the minute serious problem occur. However, an animal coming from abroad is a totally different story: I have often witnessed how - once unwanted, for whatever reasons - they are handed around, since they cannot be returned to their origin, which is mostly South or East Europe. That is the ugly downside concerning adoptions from abroad.
If all countries worldwide spayed/neutered strays thoroughly, we would hardly discuss this issue, would we? Sad but true.

My vet phoned: Platon´s poo sample shows a small amount of lungworm eggs. Right. Will start treatment tomorrow.

March 16, Tuesday
Went up to our cat shelter around noon. We discussed our website, the donations and the invoices. Before returning home, I visited Andi for a chat as well as giving him an idea what the new wildlife card game is all about. I am so glad that he will work with me on this one as well. Couldn´t think of anyone better than him! Besides, it was not hard to convince him that his house and surroundings might be perfect for releasing one or two hedgehogs in future. Ever since we started working on that hog-game together, he fell in love with the little pricklies too, hehe!
Started the lungworm treatment on Platon. He is at whopping 474 grams now.

March 17 Wednesday
Can´t even rest on my birthday: Had an urgent phone chat with the game producer in the morning, debating the event cards for *A game of spines,* plus other details.
When I thought I could get some work done before Ursel arrives for tea and cake to celebrate me, the worst thing that could happen, happened: Monty went over the fence in my backyard. I even saw him climbing up and hopping over it like a monkey. In sheer unbelief, I dropped the newspapers that I had in my hands (I was in the middle of cleaning up the hedgehog enclosures) and started calling him. Nothing.
Now panic had engulfted me completely. I went out the front door calling and searching, but nothing.

Went up to my husband´s study, from where you can see parts of the neighbouring backyards. Nothing.

Half an hour later, I saw Monty going into one of my neighbour´s carport and raced outside. Nothing. I was devastated and angry at the same time. How will I get a cat back, that is so shy and completely unfamiliar with our area? Besides, we live very close to one of the main roads with plenty of trucks whizzing by.

Mind you, it is very hard to overcome my secured fence: It is high with even a cat net on top. Most of my cats are too heavy to even climb up there, let alone getting a grip with their paws. And even IF you get up there, you have to overcome the net. Well, Monty showed that if you really want to get out, you will get out.

Called Bianca for advice. She said, the only one being able to get a hold of him, is my friend who owned him until ten days ago. Right!

End of story: She came over immediately, secured Monty (after trying to lure him in for half an hour at my open front door) and off they went. We had agreed that my place was not suitable for him, cried and hugged. No hard feelings. We gave it a try, it hadn´t worked out. That's it.

By the way: In the middle of all the chaos, Ursel arrived for my birthday and for watching the happy ending, if you could call it that.

And the happy end was only temporary. Four months later, Monty was hit by a car in front of his new adopters´ house and died right there.

March 18, Thursday
Went over to Dennis to collect my new hedgehog hibernation boxes. Since it is a three-storey-box system, I call it the "winter skyscraper". Dennis had built them exactly according to my wishes. Mind you, that is impressive work for a 16-year-old. For starters, I will move Haifa into the first floor. I need the box that she is occupying for suddenly incoming emergencies.

March 21, Sunday
Haifa has been in her new apartment for two days now. Did she wake up? Fat chance. But that's perfectly okay, since the temperatures are still chilly.
Got a text message (with photo) from Nicole. She is a friend of Ursel, and we had released a hedgehog named Tippy last year on her premises. Tippy's treatment was far from easy, since he had neurological problems, to say the least. Nicole's message showed Tippy near her feeding station, subtitled: "Look, who came back!" I was really touched, seeing the markings that identified this hog as Tippy. His reappearance explains well why we rescuers keep saying: Provide food and water, and the hoggies will stay. They are indeed a faithful lot.

March 22, Monday
Platon is slowing down, weight-wise. He offered 512 grams today. Not losing, but not really gaining anymore. Hmm. Besides, I don't like his poo. The shape of it, to be more precise. Too soft. Well, I can feel another round of treatment coming up. All my patio hedgehogs are fast asleep, for a change.
Was at my favourite vet with Ramses, in the afternoon.

I am not sure what´s bugging him, but he coughs once in a while, and I would like to exclude any possible heart problems. Nothing wrong with him, my vet said, but he is soon due for dental plaque removal.

March 24, Wednesday
Platon is back in the game! The scales showed 555 grams and he looked good. To his normal diet, I had added psyllium husks to improve his intestinal activity. Dennis and Lars had been here yesterday evenening to drop off the two remaining storeys of the winter skyscraper. Great job! That will help with my work considerably.
Did some unusual "work" during the afternoon: We have some new volunteers for our hedgehog helpline, and my task was to get them going on the phone. Not content-wise though. I was covering the psychological aspect: How to deal with difficult or rude people, without losing sight of the hedgehog that is in need.

March 25, Thursday
Went up to our cat shelter around noon. Bianca and I were fiddling about with the new website, that we had constructed. New design, new host, new everything. Takes some time to get used to it, especially when you want to work on photos and texts. Took us two hours. Looking at the result: Time well spent.

March 26, Friday
Oh my God! I uploaded my first video on instagram today. I lost at least ten thousand calories before I got that done. How to compress a file that big and for free? Eventually I got it. So check out my instagram profile.

There will be more videos - now that I know how to do it.

That video is a file from my trail cam showing Noel doing some "home improvement" in his enclosure. He was awake and having a party. So was Kandis, which surprised me. Maybe she is finally coming out of her long sleep?

Brought some cat food over to an old lady in our village who looks after strays. She is so glad about my support and for me, it is no big deal. As an animal rescuer, I sometimes get food as a donatio,n which I hand over to other people trying to help animals.

Last night I gave Platon his third and final treatment for lungworm. He lost a bit of weight, but I am not worried yet. Might be that he didn´t like the bitter meds in his food. I am sure he will make up for the loss in no time!

March 27, Saturday
Noel and his video went right through the roof! I already got 90 views for it. Unbelievable!

Ursel came over in the afternoon, for tea, cake and a chat. We discussed what to do with Platon, once his treatment is over. She suggested to move him to the outdoor enclosure and see if he wants to hibernate a little. He has gained weight again and is now at 568 grams. Good boy!

March 28, Sunday
Went to visit Pepe and Piccolo in Wacken. They are doing great, and their adopters are extremely happy with them. I was glad to see the boys in such good shape, but the main reason for my visit was to get them used to the outdoor area, together with their adopters.

So we opened the cat flap, and I went over to the other side to lure them out. As expected, Piccolo was no problem. He went through the flap and started darting up and down on the grass. Very hilarious! Pepe was the opposite: Nudged the flap a little, went through once, but turned around again after two steps. He is still very shy, but that is good. His carefulness might save him his life one day. I advised the adopters to try this every day for a few minutes and make sure they come back before dark.

March 30, Tuesday
Busy day: First, worked on a selfmade video about the development of my dice game "The temper of Titus". That took quite a while. I haven´t dealt with video making for a very long time. This is quite different from just uploading a file from the trail cam. Had to leave it half-done to go on a home visit around 40 kilometers away. The potential adopters were very nice. They had applied for a dog in Hungary. Funny coincidence: all three of us were half-breeds. Germans from the mother-side but otherwise from our daddies. In other words, a half Peruvian, a half Greek and a half Georgian were discussing a dog, that is probably also a mongrel, hehe! On my way back, I stopped at the local cemetery to fill some clay bowls with water.
Noel´s video has climbed up to 124 views. Wow! What can I say apart from thank you!
The adopters of Piccolo and Pepe texted me: Pepe has not returned home from his outside adventure. They were upset. I tried to calm them down, but to be honest, I was worried myself.

These days, the weather is warm and sunny, and the curious little bugger had been trapped indoors for five weeks now. Of course he is enjoying himself now in the fresh spring air. Good for him, worrysome for us.

March 31, Wednesday
It is even warmer today and still no sight of Pepe! His adopters are worried to death by now. I am so sorry for them and hope that this will come to a happy end.
Went to the adjoining village´s graveyard to fill up the bowls there.
Still no sign of Pepe. Talked to the adopters over the phone and told them what to do next: Go out at night with a headlamp and treats. It is always easier to catch your cats at nighttime. You hear them better and vice versa. Plus, they emerge quicker when there is no noise or traffic.
Got a call back from the adopters at 11 p.m.: Pepe is back! They found him in a side street close to their home. I am so thrilled - and so are they!

April 3, Saturday
I have been busy working on my Titus-video over the last days. It´s only a 60-second-piece for instagram, but still so time-consuming! Besides, I didn´t like my first draft and started all over again. Sigh!
In the meantime, Noel´s video has passed the 160 views and the new video showing Platon has passed the 100. This instagram thing starts being fun.
Speaking of Platon: I have moved him to an enclosure on my patio today. He weighed 607 grams, and I think he was eager to get some fresh air.

Of course, I had the trail cam ready to capture any of his monkey tricks during the night.

My husband and I finished the drawings for the wildlife cards today. They don't look too bad. Next step is playing with testplayers. I have a dejà vu though. Last year, exactly the same problem: No meetings, no game sessions. It will be hard to tempt anyone into playing a game with the Corona numbers rising like crazy. Damn!

April 5, Monday
Platon: 114 views. Noel: 173 views. Yeehaw!
Loaded up the video about the making of "The temper of Titus" on instagram, at last. I guess, next night I will be dreaming of .mov, .avi., .wav and .mpg-files including converting and compressing. Glad, it's done!
Went over to Ursel's for tea, cake and chat. She still has one hedgehog under surveillance: Sieglinde. Treatment done but she must put on weight. Ursel asked me to come back on Wednesday, since Paddle-Bianca's claws are too long. They need a cut. And Ursel wants me to assist. Sure thing!

April 7, Wednesday
As planned, I went over to Ursel's to assist with Paddle-Bianca's claw-cutting. Well, at least we tried. Bianca, as always, was in a foul mood, puffing and huffing and not at all cooperating. She is both the beauty and the beast! We gave up after three claws and Ursel said, she will try again some other time. Probably at the vet's with a light sedation. Mind you, Bianca does not only huff; she bites too!

Found hog poo in my garden. The first poo this year! Don't worry. It is very typical for a hog fosterer to get excited over poo in the garden. I wonder which of my outside hogs has finally woken up: Alfred, Buddha, Doron, Ebo, Faunus, Gandhi, Ipanema, Jade or Leander? I hope they are all safe and will make a re-appearance at my feeding stations, which are already full of food, waiting to be chomped.

April 8, Thursday
Drove over to my cat shelter. Did the invoices with Bianca and the cash register accounting. There was still time for a chat, and we really enjoyed that. With spring coming up and bringing kittens, there will be no time for private chatting any more. Before going home, I stopped by at Andi´s house to discuss the latest development of our hog-game. Since it is in production, there is not much we can do any more, apart from waiting for the result. We are both very excited.

April 9, Friday
Received the result of the poo samples from Mozart, Kandis and Noel: all negative! Wow. That means they are clean and whenever they are ready, they can be released. But not yet. Temperatures are still too low.

April 11, Sunday
Since I found more hog poo in the feeding station two days ago, I set up the trail cam and reviewed the footage, consisting of three files, this morning. File one: neighbour´s cat. File two: nothing at all. File three: a hedgehog running out of the picture. Hmpf! Will try again in two days.

April 12, Monday
Went to Hamburg for two things. First, stopping at our family graveyard to fill up the water bowls. Second, seeing Beate, who lives nearby and had brought two hedgehogs to me last year. She is one of the hedgehog taxis that drives for our helpline. I met her first last November, when she handed Mozart over, who was found in an area, that was not suitable for him to go back, due to lack of natural surroundings. I agreed with Beate, that Mozart should be released in her garden, since she loves hedgehogs and has feeding stations, water bowls and even a trail cam. We had a drink and a chat in her garden, and yes, I decided to release Mozart here. I might bring one of my female hogs as well. Beate would just flip, if she saw hoglets on her trail cam one day.
Got a list from one of the shelters, I do the follow-ups for, over the weekend. Due to Covid, we don´t physically visit, but ring them up. So I started the list this evening with a very nice lady, that got a dog from Spain. From all she told me, I could hear that everything is in super order there!

April 13, Tuesday
Leander is back!
I watched the footage of the trail cam and found Leander on it. He was the very last hedgehog I saw in my garden last year before winter arrived. I recognized the markings, formed in shape of the letter L. I mark all my hedgehogs according to their names with non-poisonous paint. God, was I chuffed to see him enter the feeding station!

My cam revealed that neighbour´s cat obviously watched him too, which gave me a good laugh. Of course I loaded the video up on my instagram account. Took Ramses to another vet in order to find out whether anything else is wrong with him, but the vet only said the same: He is due for dental plaque removal. Well then. Got an appointment for just that in two weeks.

April 15, Thursday
Everything is very quiet these days. All my patio hoggies are still asleep, apart from Mozart and Platon. The hedgehog helpline is also very quiet: Just 7-10 calls per day. This will increase enormously, once the weather switches to summer mode. I fill my spare time with those phone follow-ups and so far, I only had nice adopters that told me how happy they were with their dogs.

April 17, Saturday
Ursel was here, for tea and cake. I wanted her to have a look at Mozart, because he lost some spines. It could be the normal loss and regrowth that occurs when they are young, but I thought those were a bit too many. Ursel agreed and also found a small wound on his nose. Since I will be away for a few days soon, I am supposed to bring Mozart over to her, so that she can start the treatment.
He gained a lot of weight over the last months. That´s something, at least.

April 18, Sunday
Cycled over to the cemetery, that is five kilometers away, to fill up the water bowls. The weather is warm and no rain in sight. All bowls empty.

April 19, Monday
Handed Mozart over to Ursel. She gave him the first antibiotic (out of three) and will think up a supplemental nutrition for his skin problem. Mozart was swapped for "Crumb", a hedgehog who doesn´t need any treatment and is fast asleep, according to Ursel. When I arrived home with Crumb, I realized that I forgot to ask Ursel whether it is a male or a female.

April 20, Tuesday
Crumb, who is male, as Ursel told me, was certainly awake during the night. So were Noel, Kandis and Platon. To my great delight, Platon has gained weight and showed 792 grams. Brilliant! Haifa and Octavia are still peacefully asleep.
Filled up the water bowls at our local cemetery. Also dry and empty. Poor hogs!

April 26, Monday
Long time, no write! Came back from a short holiday yesterday evening. My hogsitter did a decent job while I was away. Nothing has changed much: Noel and Platon are still the ones that are awake during the night. Not much movement in the girls´ enclosures. However, their time is nearly up.

April 27, Tuesday
Swapped Crumb for Mozart again. Ursel told me that
Mozart was doing fine. I just have to continue the meds
concerning his skin issues for another week. He has
gained weight in the meantime: 960 grams. Sounds
good to me. On the way back home I filled the water
bowls at our cemetery. In case you get bored by me
writing this all the time: Imagine, that I do this every
week until autumn. Animal lives depend on this task,
especially during hot summer periods. Please do this
also, whenever you visit a cemetery. Even if you don't
see them – you can help our wildlife!

April 28, Wednesday
Took Ramses to the vet for his dental plaque removal.
And, on my way home, filled more water bowls at the
cemetery in the neighbouring village. Not one drop of
water was left in them. Really scary! No wonder, we
rescuers get so many dehydrated hedgehogs.
Collected Ramses in the afternoon. All went smooth,
they told me at the vet´s, however, they had to pull one
rotten tooth. I am glad that this is over now. I remember
last time very well, when I had to bring him in for his
dental treatment: The next day, when he was allowed to
eat again, he wouldn´t, due to severe pain. That resulted
in dehydration and he collapsed. I was so tense that day,
that I swore to myself, that I will always ask the vet for
pain killers, next time one of my cats has to get any sort
of dental surgery. Now let´s see how Ramses behaves
tomorrow. I am on full alert!

April 29, Thursday
Collected the trail cam and viewed the footage. A hog rescue station, that I am friends with, had asked me for some footage on how hedgehogs use the rat flaps when entering the feeding station. And since Leander is around every night, I gave it a try. And yes, he did the absolute perfect entry through the flaps. My friend is very happy with the footage!
Gave Ramses some pain killer around noon, since he was reluctant to eat. In the evening though, he ate a little. So far, so good.

April 30, Friday
Ramses is behaving and eating normally, so obviously he has no major after effects from the surgery. I am so glad.
Meanwhile, there is not much to report from my six hedgehogs on the patio: The females are asleep and the males are awake. I put Platon on the scales today: 822 grams. Super!
I have gradually started arranging their releases by calling up the finders that had allowed the hoggies to be put back in their gardens. I will start with Mozart and Kandis end of next week. Or so I hope.

May 2, Sunday
My good friend Ursel was here for a quick chat and picking up some meds, she ran out of. We discussed the forthcoming releases of our hedgehogs. The show will start after next weekend, with night temperatures being tolarable for our spiny friends.

May 3, Monday
Number seven arrived today: A girl from our region found a diurnal hog and brought it over. I tried to examine it, but it curled up so tight, that I gave that a miss for now, since it had no obvious injuries. She told me that it had eaten plenty of food at hers yesterday, so I wasn't too concerned. I put the spiny ball on the scales: 726 grams. After I tucked it into a prepared box, I set up the trail cam for possible night activities. Well, let's see.

May 4, Tuesday
May the fourth be with you, friends. But now back to the pricklies: My new arrival didn't budge one inch! The cam filmed absolutely nothing. Food was untouched too, logically. Is it back in hibernation? Well, no worries - I keep it under close surveillance.
Ha! Caught it eating, so it is hungry after all. No wonder: from what I could see, it is awfully thin. I hope, I can help the poor mite.
I sent off Platon's poo sample today. And started collecting poo from number seven.

May 5, Wednesday
Since I saw it stirring in the cage, I picked up number seven and put it on the scales: 751 grams. Then removed some ticks and checked it through: Aha, male. The finder wanted the name "Pit" for him, so Pit went back into his enclosure and started eating immediately. I think, he is doing quite well.
A dreadful storm (with heavy rain) is passing over Northern Europe today. I put on my wellies and checked on my patio hogs. All in order.

45

I filled up their bowls and hurried back inside. The ladies are still asleep, but even the boys have kept everything tidy.

May 7, Friday
Went over to Ursel with Pit, who had gained weight, so that she can check him. And Ursel wouldn´t be Ursel if she didn´t find out whatever was wrong with Pit. First, she found five very tiny ticks, that I have overlooked. Then she opened his mouth and showed me, that there was an infection going on. She cleaned and rinsed it thoroughly. During examination of his belly, Ursel spotted an abscess on his throat. Oh dear! "He is not in a good condition", she said, frowning and wanted me to start antibiotic treatment right away. I started giving him the first shot in the evening. Minimum is five rounds, every two days, my teacher ordered. I must admit that I was a bit crestfallen: I had hoped that the underweight would be the only problem. You see, that makes hedgehog fostering such a delicate job!

May 8, Saturday
First official testplay of the wildlife cardgame with a big family having three kids. We played with three, four and five people, plus a variation of cards to find out what works best. That was really interesting and I learned a lot. Before anyone gets upset: We were all wearing surgical masks.
On my way back, I stopped at our cemetery to fill the water bowls. Weather forecast announced that tomorrow will be the first real hot day this year.

May 9, Sunday

Pit got his second shot of antibiotics today. With dismay I noticed that he has not gained weight, but lost a bit. Now what? Went over to Ursel to take some photographs of Paddle-Bianca, before Ursel releases her later this evening. We also discussed Pit´s situation, and Ursel will try to get a better antibiotic for him when she sees her vet tomorrow.

Don´t know why, but I feel really gloomy today. Even the smallest problems irritate me. Maybe too many things happening at the same time? Hopefully, my mood gets better, once the releasing period has started.

May 10, Monday

Big day for Mozart and Kandis! I prepared them for release: checking, weighing and marking. And off they went: to Beate, our hedgehog taxi. She had everything ready: feeding station and water bowls. Her garden is very natural, so they will have a good life here.

Before returning home, I stopped at our family cemetery to fill up the water bowls We have 25 degrees today!

Received the result of Platon´s poo sample in the evening: Coccidia and very few lungworm eggs. Will start treatment tomorrow.

Bit of a punch in the face, when the lady, that brought Haifa last year, told me that she won´t take her back, because I had collected her in the middle of hibernation (see February 15). She is still sulky about that. I gently tried to explain why I did what I did. A hog in supervised hibernation has to be checked daily, including food and water supply, since it is very likely that they wake up once in a while during that period.

Besides, it can be tricky to keep their enclosure and bedroom box dry, if you are not experienced. And mould is the last thing we need for a hog in hibernation. Well, things are as they are, and I will find a good home for her. In hindsight, I thought, it was probably better that Haifa would not return to that place. That family was not really motivated to learn anything.

May 11, Tuesday
Had the trail cam out last night. The footage was fantastic: Saw Gandhi (my fattest outdoor hog) and Jade several times at the feeding station in my carport. Plus two cats. There was a traffic jam around midnight, when they all came to dine at the same time. I saved one picture for instagram.
Did a home visit for two cats in the afternoon: Lovely girl! Definitely a green light from my side. Stopped at Ursel´s on my way back, since I needed some meds for Pit. Ursel told me, that Paddle-Bianca is still sleeping in her shed, though released. But not in her own box! She moved in to a male hog. "Oh, a romance", I giggled. Ursel wanted to show me the box with Bianca and her lover, but only the male hog was in there. Ursel frowned, checked the other boxes and found Bianca in an adjoining box.
"Maybe they had an argument", I grinned and Ursel closed the shed laughing.

May 12, Wednesday
Got the result of Pit´s poo sample: negative. Good! That means that I can concentrate on his pharyngitis. At least, he is eating well and gaining weight. Next week, I will take him in to the vet.

May 14, Friday
Finally - Haifa is awake! She has been eating wet cat food for two days. Put her on the scales: 638 grams. She lost a bit, but that´s quite normal for a hog hibernating that long without a break. I will stuff her with nice meals and simultaneously collect her droppings for analysis. Now waiting for Octavia. She is the last one to wake up and get checked.
Went to the vet in the morning and obtained the new antibiotic for Pit.

May 15, Saturday
Big day for Noel. We released him in the garden of a family in our neighbouring village. They look after a lot of wild animals (bees, birds, you name it) and their garden is huuuuuuge! Noel got the jackpot, really. I am sure he will be more than okay here. I told them that I will bring Haifa too, in around two weeks. After saying our good-byes there, my hubby and I went over to another family with a hog-friendly garden. They offered to supplement food and water as well. Yes, this might be suitable for Octavia. We will see.
Pit is still eating well, and his new antibiotic seems to work. He is awfully friendly and trusts me. It will be hard to release him in about three weeks.
Sent off poo samples: Pit´s again, since I didn´t fully trust the first one. And Haifa´s, who produces her first poo now. This time, I sent the samples to Jenny, the head of our hedgehog emergency network. She is an expert and no parasite will escape her eyes for sure!

May 16, Sunday
And here goes another one: Big day for Platon, who will return to Glückstadt this afternoon. Scales showed 902 grams, and he is fit and ready to rumble. That was another brilliant release: The finders were really nice and experienced with hedgehogs. They had everything ready for him and even gave me some money plus a bottle of wine ("You had expenses, didn´t you?"). We agreed that they will get Octavia as well, since their garden is very large and natural.

May 17, Monday
No more releases for a while (next are Haifa and Octavia, the only ones left, apart from Pit), but important day for Pit, since he has an appointment at the vet´s today, due to the growing abscess. Result: He is in for surgery tomorrow.

May 18, Tuesday
Brought Pit in around noon and collected him around five. The vet told me that, after having cut into the abscess, loads of pus came out. Meaning, I will have to drain it daily. Well, I was prepared for that, but how the hell do I drain an abscess on the throat with the hedgehog being fully awake?
By the way: The lady from Lübeck (with hedgehog Willy, see February 20) has contacted me: Willy has obviously gone back to hibernation and wouldn´t eat. I gave her some advice, asked her to monitor his weight and keep me posted on any development. Besides, I wanted her to collect poo, the minute he wakes up and eats again. The rule stands: Never release a hog, you had over winter, without a final poo check!

May 19, Wednesday
Pit had been eating well overnight, but as I was trying to find the cut for the draining treatment this morning, I couldn´t find anything. Besides, Pit was worming his way out of my hands. I was afraid of hurting him, if I continue trying to look for the cut. An abscess so near the carotid artery is a lot different than one near a leg or on the back. I wouldn´t dare to make a mistake that costs Pit his old life. Consequently, I phoned Ursel, who is way better in this. We agreed, that I will drive over later, with my patient.

Used my noon break to fill water bowls at our cemetery.

Later at Ursel´s: She examined Pit and frowned: The cut is too small, she said, draining will be difficult. Nevertheless, she started the drainage only to find out that no pus was coming out. "The left side is soft", she explained, "but I am worried about the right side. Another abscess might be in progress there." Ursel gave me some meds (including pain killers, telling me that she was surprised that the vet didn´t give me any) and home I went.

May 20, Thursday
Good news: Pit has 1.053 grams! Bad news: I still don´t know how to continue treatment on his abscess. Or to be more precise: Which antibiotic is the best for him? I have gathered several opinions from different rescues, and I have to make up my mind. The thing is: Changing an antibiotic can cause resistances. I will stick to the one, that he has been on for the last five days, since that seemed to have worked until now. You see, antibiotics are not all the same.

Some are good for shallow wounds, others for lung problems or bone fractures, some for anything that has to do with the jaw or mouth. Therefore, you cannot just give anything you like.

May 22, Saturday
Result of poo samples came in. Haifa: nothing. Pit: bit of lungworm larvae, bit of capillaria. Okay, will treat that, once the abscess is under control.
Went up to our cat shelter in the evening. We had dinner together with our staff plus husbands. Was a very nice change, since - due to the pandemic - we haven´t met up in a group for quite some time. So far, no emergency kittens have arrived, but that can change any minute in this season. We are prepared.

May 23, Sunday
Ursel was here for tea and cake. She really liked one of the birthday presents I gave her: Big picture of Paddle-Bianca in her garden. I had taken that photograph some weeks ago. We had a nice chat, and of course she checked on Pit. He is doing well, she claimed, after examining him. I was honestly chuffed about that. Besides, Pit had fabulous 1.073 grams to present this morning.

May 24, Monday
Had the cam out, with view onto the dry food station in my carport. The number of hogs is increasing! I saw Gandhi, Jade and Ebo. Gandhi had an argument with Jade around 3 a.m. The video showed her balling up and Gandhi pushing and rolling her under my car. He has such a temper. Sigh!

May 26, Wednesday
Death day of my cats Picasso and Trinity (2016/5/26 and 2020/5/26). I still mourn them so much. Losing Pica five years ago was the worst thing that happened to me in my entire life. I had never felt so numb before - ever!

May 27, Thursday
These are really busy days, and I can hardly keep up with the diary. Let´s see, what happened over the last three days? Oh yes, I started doing follow-up calls again for shelter dogs, that had been adopted last year. Had the cam out again, this time above the wet food station. Hmm, saw some hogs alright, and with my markings, but couldn´t tell who was who. Have to set up the cam again next week at a different angle.
Meanwhile Pit is doing fine. He is at 1.150 grams now, and Ursel and myself had a lot of discussions how to go on. The abscess seems to have disappeared. His teeth are clean too, his throat doesn´t show any signs of infection any more. So I guess I can drop the antibiotic soon.
Released Haifa this afternoon. She went to the big beautiful garden where I had released Noel two weeks ago.
Octavia is still asleep. I had checked on her last night, to see whether she is still breathing. Hogs can die during hibernation, for various reasons. Octavia, however, huffed loudly at me, when I gently touched her spines. That was all I wanted to hear. Since the weather is lousy (haven´t seen a May that was so cold and rainy ever before), I can´t blame her.

A high pressure area will approach Europe from tomorrow on. My hope is, that Octavia will finally get up then.

May 28, Friday
Ramses, after sitting there, had left urine stains on the couch recently. Went to the vet with him. The vet couldn´t find anything wrong with my soulmate. So we guess, that it is caused by stress. Plus, he howls sometimes, at nighttime, while he drags his favorite blanket through the house. He is not happy, that´s obvious. Therefore, I had applied for a cat from Belarus last week, that might be a nice match for him. Now I am waiting for a reply.
Haifa´s adopters had sent a photo taken by their cam this morning. There she was, outside her cardboard box, in which I brought her over. But she went in again, for sleeping, they told me. Yes, hedgehogs do that sometimes, before they build their own nest. Seems, she is not in a hurry to explore her new surroundings. Mind you, that box of hers is right beside the feeding station. And she is a hungry one. Go figure!

May 30, Sunday
Re-visited Pepe and Piccolo in Wacken. I had really missed them and was so happy that they both came running when I called them. Amira and Lucas had prepared tea, and I had baked a cake this morning. The weather was lovely, and we were sitting outside on their patio watching the two cats racing across the garden or scuffling and rolling about. I thanked this awesome couple again for letting me see them once in a while. This is the jackpot - can´t say that often enough!

May 31, Monday
Went to the vet with Pit, who had moved to my patio two days ago. Pit was awfully excited about the move and sniffed the fresh air with his nose up high. Maybe his hormones have kicked in, and he was aware of Octavia, who is still sleeping in the enclosure on top of him. Anyway, the vet thinks that Pit is fit enough to be released. So I made an appointment with his finders for Wednesday.

June 1, Tuesday
Shock! Jenny announced that the hedgehog helpline will be shut down at the end of this month. That makes all of us, working for the line, very sad, since it means that a lot of hedgehogs will not be helped in future. However, I understand her reasoning: Most rescues are already full and some have quit. Again, the reason for the latter is money: Nearly all of them treat and nurse hedgehogs on a voluntary basis and spend an awful lot of personal dough on them. Finders, often not aware of this expensive task, donate little or nothing. So, everybody´s running out of money! It is a shame and makes me very angry, but not in direction to the rescues, hell no! I blame our politicians. The state is wasting so much money on useless shit and wouldn´t even ask the citizens if they concur, but when it comes to people, who sacrifice their private lives and their money, they are left alone. Honestly, I go ape, whenever I think about this. The voluntary work done by any rescuer, fosterer or environmentalist is vital for the well-being of this planet and should be supported. Fullstop!

But that was not all today. When I was roaming around in our garden shed, I found Jade sitting underneath a shelf. Now what? I scooped her up and brought her in. She was bleeding somewhere. Only a little, but still! And in she went, into one of the enclosures. Her weight is good: In November she had 715 and today 1.060 grams. Well, I will see what I can do for her.

But that was still not all. When I thought the day was over, sitting at the dinner table, the phone went: my local vet. He had a hedgehog in a very bad condition. I left my half-eaten plate and went over to collect what I thought was a dying hedgehog. But I still find myself too inexperienced to tell him straight away, that he should put him down. The hog had massive flystrike around the eyes and breathing difficulties. No, that´s an understatement. He was gasping for air so desperately that it made my heart bleed. He had 590 grams and was an adult. I raced over to Ursel, and we treated him with what we had, but around 11 p.m. he closed his eyes for good. What a shitty day!

June 2, Wednesday
Packed day again. First went over to Pit´s finders to release him. Lovely rural area, no traffic. And he knows his way around, since he came from there. That is the ideal situation for any hedgehog, plus the supplemental food and water, of course.

Then I drove up to our cat shelter, did the invoices with Bianca and discussed the current shelter issues, which included a new cat, that had been dropped at our shelter: pregnant and just huuuuge! Bianca calls her "Big Noodle", and we are awaiting her babies any minute.

Besides, I got introduced to our new shelter dog, that Bianca had adopted, some kind of German shepherd, named Amira. She is still very shy, but loves cuddles.

On my way back home, I stopped at one of my cemeteries to fill the water bowls. I was a bit reluctant with my work, because I spotted a woman that was tidying a grave with a rake nearby. And I know I am not always welcome with my helping the wildlife. Working for animal welfare also means making enemies sometimes. Anyway, I started on the other side and hoped for the best. When I came down again, the woman called over. If it was me, who keeps filling the bowls, she wanted to know. I explained my mission and my hedgehog fostering to her, and she was really thrilled. She is also an animal lover and told me, that she was wondering for some time who the ghost was, that attended to those bowls. We had a nice conversation and that lady totally made my day.
Coming home, I dived into my daily chores and, of course, checked on Jade. She had eaten well over night. But on a closer look, I saw that she had mites! Started treatment today. Besides, found out that Jade was a male hog. Well then, Monsieur Jade.

June 3, Thursday
The day started with a home-check for adopting an animal. But this time, I was not the one who did the checking, but the possible adopter! And it was not a physical visit, but a video chat, concerning the cat in Belarus, that I had applied for. The conversation went very well, and they have no doubt that my place is the right home for Phoebe!

Went to our family cemetery in Hamburg to fill up the water bowls. Then I collected two new feeding stations from Dennis. He had built them for Ursel, and I offered to drive them up, so that Ursel wouldn´t have to do the long drive. I thought I owe that to her, since she spent a lot of extra time with the dying hedgehog on Tuesday. Ursel was very happy about the new feeding stations - she adores Dennis´ work just as much as I do!
Late at night, we buried the hedgehog near the forest. With a flower and a name. Rest in peace, Quincy.

June 4, Friday
Treatment finished. Bathed Monsieur Jade (that was part of the mite treatment) and, with dusk coming up, released him in my garden, where he belongs.

June 5, Saturday
Had the cam out last night. Saw Jade, Ebo and Gandhi.
Will have to bring Octavia, who is still not eating properly, over to Ursel´s later this afternoon. Ursel will take care of her (and find the reason why she wouldn't eat) while I am on holiday for a week. I hope that at least on Texel (a Dutch island), there will be no hedgehogs in need. But I will have my rescue kit with me, just in case.
After having left Octavia with Ursel, I stopped by at the place where we had buried Quincy. All was in order there. Nice, peaceful place.
Late at night, I got a call from the hedgehog helpline: An injured hog was found around 35 kilometers away from me. Yikes. I will be on holiday from tomorrow on, so I can´t take it.

Spent half the night organizing a place for the hog, but found a solution in the end. More details, when I return home.

June 12, Saturday
On our way back home from Texel, we stopped at *Felida Big Cat Sanctuary*. I had made an appointment with them, before we started our holiday. Two years ago, I had been here for an interview with them, so you find a chapter about their work in my book *Pfotenengel*. *Felida* is a Dutch project by Four Paws, rescuing mistreated and caged wild animals, which are brought over here and taken care for, to live a decent rest life and hopefully forget what people did to them.
It was thrilling to be back here and see Dehli, the Tigress again. Sadly, most of the animals that I had seen back then, had died in the meantime.
I was introduced to Bobby and Ivan-Asen (I knew the latter already from my last visit), two lions, that were very relaxed and sun-bathing. Dehli, however, was quite excited, since she likes humans, and was pacing and greeting us. It was so awesome to be back here - what a fantastic way to end an already fantastic holiday!

June 14, Monday
Collected Octavia from Ursel, who had nursed her well during my absence. Brought her over to Glückstadt for final release. That´s the place where Platon had come from and was released again. Now he has some female company.

June 15, Tuesday

Got a call from Hamburg: very weak and underweight hog. Ordered them to one of my vets immediately. First had to deal with Monk, my black cat, who got his vaccination and check-up today, including blood test. I expected him to be agressive, since he had very few vet visits so far, but none of it! He was sweet as pie and so easy to handle, I couldn´t believe my eyes!

Collected the poorly hog in the evening. Ursel came around and took over, since Erica arrived at the same time: She was the hog that I had organized away due to my holiday. Erica is eating well, has a large cut below her throat (probably got tangled in a wiremesh fence) and a dodgy front leg. That calls for a long treatment.

What a busy day.

June 16, Wednesday

Had the cam out last night. I think I could make out Doron. And definitely Ebo. His marking was chrystal-clear. And one hog, I couldn´t recognize. Hmm, where are the others, I wonder?

Ursel called: the hog didn´t make it. Oh, bummer! But he won´t go without a name. Rest in peace, Ruslan.

Vet called: Monk´s blood sample is perfectly okay. So next in line will be his tooth treatment. But that will have to wait until July.

Another hog was brought to me in the afternoon. A female! Named her Shannon. The woman, who found her, said, that she was eating well. I examined her. Okay, her left eye has a bad infection, maybe she got hit. But apart from that: good skin, warm body, no wounds, perfect spines. And she showed an interest in the dry food immediately. Good.

June 17, Thursday
Had a funny feeling when I woke up around 4 a.m. and went downstairs to check on Shannon. She hadn´t eaten anything, plus, she was wobbly, when I touched her. That set my alarm off, and I started subcut fluids right away. Though her body was warm and our outside temperatures were around 20 degrees at this time of the day, I offered her a heatpad, that she could leave any time. Continued with the fluids when I got up again around 8:30. Then phoned another hog expert to debate what I should get done with her when I go to the vet later. When I checked Shannon again, she had died. Just like that. 9:15 a.m. I was completely devastated. I arranged to bring her to the lab tomorrow, because I want to know what went wrong, or, more precisely: What was wrong from the start! I cried the whole way up to our cat shelter where Bianca hugged me heartily. We went to the vet with "Big Noodle", our pregnant cat. Everything is grand with her. Did some shelter work and talked a lot. When I drove home, I cried again. Stopped once to fill the water bowls at one of my cemeteries (sunny, 30 degrees, everybody thirsty). What a horrible day!

June 18, Friday
Saw Buddha and Gandhi on the trail cam at the dry feeding station.
Went over to the lab with Shannon for autopsy. The lab is about 45 kilometers away from my home. They are really nice people, and the drive is very peaceful. It is always hard to do this, but so necessary. I will spread the report among other hog rescues, so that, hopefully, all of us can learn something from the final analysis.

Erica is doing well, gaining weight. She passed the 800 grams. However, I am worried about her front leg. She still doesn´t want to use it. Ursel will have to do an assessment soon.

June 19, Saturday
Went to Ursel´s with Erica. Ursel had a look at her cut and gave me some advice for further treatment. And then we let her "walk" in the grass. She was hopping more than walking, but Ursel believes, that she is willing to use that front leg of hers, that all depends on the neurological progress, and that it requires a lot of patience on my side. That doesn´t sound too bad to me.

June 21, Monday
Just read on Facebook that Ivan-Asen has died! The lion we visited nine days ago at *Felida*. That really broke my heart. I am so blessed to have met him twice. Now and two years ago. May he rest in peace and never ever be forgotten!

June 22, Tuesday
Received the pathology report on Shannon. She had a massive amount of different bacteria including salmonella! The poor mite must have been desperate for food and eaten something bad. It seems that salmonella is something that is increasing also among hedgehogs. With the current heat, it is not a good idea to put out wet food during daytime, for sure! My hogs get their wet food after dusk, and I collect the bowls first thing in the morning.

June 24, Thursday
Congratulations!
"Big Noodle" finally had her babies, three in total. And they are huge too! Bianca, who was quite worried during the long pregnancy, is very relieved now. Did a follow-up for an animal shelter on a cat. Everything was nice and orderly there and the people very pleasant. Since that place was very close to Ursel's, I stopped by and delivered some meds, that she needed for her hedgehogs, plus collecting my trail cam that I had left with her. After a nice chat with Ursel, who was in excellent spirits, I stopped once again at our cemetery to fill up some water bowls. Today´s missions: complete!

June 26, Saturday
Got a call from a hog rescue nearby: Could I take over a hedgehog that was found and not looking good? Well, yes. Now that was the hugest abscess, that I had ever seen on a hog! Poor thing. He (named him Tetris) could hardly walk or stretch. He got an antibiotic shot plus some pain meds and, of course, food and water. The lady that brought him over said, that she had fed him with bird food. I took a deep breath and told her that bird food is very wrong for hedgehogs. She felt awfully sorry, and I assured her, that this is a mistake many people make. Hedgehogs are carnivores, and it is quite dangerous to feed them fruit, nuts, vegetables and the likes. The lady was really lovely, and I am glad that Tetris, treatment being over, may return to her garden. In the meantime, Ursel was showing up, for tea, cake and checking on Erica. Erica´s cut has healed nicely, she said.

Then we let Erica walk in my back garden, to see how her lame front leg is doing. Ursel was quite satisfied and believes that Erica might fully recover, but it will still take time. We also viewed the footage from the trail cam (which I had left at Ursel´s, couple of days ago), and Ursel laughed at realizing, that it was mainly the same hedgehog returning to the feeding station over and over again. Mind you, my outdoor hedgehogs are seldom coming at all these days: I keep throwing away the wet food. The mating seems to be more important than the eating right now.

June 27, Sunday
Checked on Tetris during the night and in the morning: He is eating a little of the wet food, which is stuffed with pain meds and nutritional supplements. Ursel had said that the abscess has to be cut as soon as possible, so I will make an appointment at the vet´s first thing in the morning. Come on, Tetris, just one more day. Hang in!

June 28, Monday
Went to the vet with Tetris. He had 867 grams today. That´s 5 grams more than on Saturday, which is not satisfying. At the vet's, they were really busy today, so I had to leave Tetris there and go home. They will call me, when he is ready to be collected, so now I am glued to my cellphone. They called in the early evening and I drove over. The pus that had come out of the abscess had a weight of 120 grams, they said. Jesus! I took him home and gave him some food which he immediately ate. So far, so good.

Filled water bowls at two different cemeteries, in between the vet visits.

June 29, Tuesday
Went over to Ursel´s and we rinsed the abscess. Ursel frowned: Why did the vet only open the big abscess below and not the small one on the back? She advised me to see another vet tomorrow and handed me a list, what should be done and what medicine we still need for Tetris. At least, we have a plan now.

June 30, Wednesday
Went over to the other vet in the morning. The second abscess was opened (more pus), and Tetris received some antibiotics. The vet also rinsed everything and cut off some loose parts around the big hole, just like Ursel advised. Tetris was very brave (again!) and gained weight, which delighted me enormously.
Today is the last day of our hedgehog helpline. I will do some calls too in the evening. Then, there will be a longer break, in which we will try to think of a better system to help people.

Yikes! My last call for the hedgehog helpline was an awful one! The finders were not willing to secure the poorly hog they spotted in a park and found zillions of excuses for not doing anything. They left it there to die slowly. Those are the moments, when I feel so damn helpless.

July 1, Thursday
Went to Ursel´s with both Erica and Tetris. Erica will stay with her and move to an outdoor enclosure, since she is fit enough to train her leg outside, and she was already suffering from cabin fever.
Tetris was examined, and Ursel said that the antibiotic given is surely not strong enough, though all the vets we talked to, said that it should be. But Ursel knows better! She showed me the pus that started building up again around the abscess´ opening. We have to leave it for a day, since you can´t just change antibiotics like and whenever you want. But from tomorrow on, he will get the right one. We rinsed the two wounds thoroughly and removed any pus or dead tissue. I am so glad that he has gained weight again. My Tetris is a fighter, and we are standing at his side!

July 2, Friday
And again at Ursel´s. We flushed the wounds, removed some fresh pus and gave antibiotics. And found mites! Well, I will erase the mite problem in the evening, that is not our major concern. Ursel was satisfied with him, and we let him rest. Before I left, I had a look at Erica´s new enclosure: oh wow, she must be happy in there. It is in Ursel's garden, roofed of course, and she can exercise her leg in the grass. I watched her wobble around, and I am convinced that she will be fine again - it just takes time. With dodgy legs, always.

July 3, Saturday
Once more at Ursel´s: Treated Tetris and left him with her until I will be back. He is in the best hands, I have nothing to worry about.

Filled up the water bowls at our cemetery.

July 4, Sunday
What an unusual day with an unusual visit at our cat shelter: The "Westcoastbikers", a motorcycle gang, visited our shelter today. Once a year, they collect money for a small charity organisation and this year, they chose us. Bianca and I served drinks and showed them around. Luckily, we already had some new kitten arrivals, and everyone flipped at their sight. Great day that was. I am so thankful, that there are still people out there, caring about us small shelters that do not get any offical donations from the state or otherwise.

July 7, Wednesday
Bought some meds at the Black Sea for our hedgehogs back home, that I wouldn´t be able to get in Germany without a major fuss. I am glad that East Europe is not so strict, law-wise.

July 11, Sunday
Stopped by at the sister of my sister-in-law in Istanbul who had found an abandoned kitten and is struggling to rear it. Showed her how to hold and feed it and gave her all my knowledge about temperature of the baby milk, feeding intervals, toiletting, you name it. I hope that she will be successful, since it is not easy to bottlefeed, if you have never done it before. Besides, with animal babies, things can go wrong so fast, if you lack the experience. We will stay in touch, and I will try to help her as much as I can. However, bad timing, since I will return to Germany tomorrow.

July 13, Tuesday
Went over to Ursel in the afternoon, to see how Erica and Tetris are doing. Erica had digged her way out of her enclosure while I was away, but Ursel is not really worried. If she can do that, then her leg is okay! Erica wanted her freedom so bad, and there was actually no reason to keep her any longer. Besides, it is not allowed to keep a wild animal, once the treatment is over. Well, have a happy life in Ursel´s garden, Erica!
With Tetris, things are not looking too bad either! The big abscess has healed fantastically- you can hardly see it any more. Ursel is a true wizzard! She will keep him a little while longer to observe the remains of the abscess, before he can leave. She has no other hedgehogs right now, so that´s no problem. I am glad, that Tetris can return to his finder´s garden soon.
My produced hedgehog games ("A game of spines") arrived today. 350 of them! We were really thrilled, but soon discovered, that the plastic feet for the hedgehog game figures were missing. Oh, no! I will have to call the production company first thing in the morning tomorrow. That sucks.

July 14, Wednesday
Was at our cat shelter today. Went through the latest invoices, checked on the "noodle-family" (plus trying to take pics of Big Noodle and her three babies, which are a lively lot!) and discussed the latest entries, also known as kittens. Bianca gave me one to tame, that came in yesterday night. A female with 944 grams. She will stay "on box", as we say, until she is successfully socialized with humans.

July 15, Thursday
Very busy day: First, dropped Monk off at the vet´s for plaque removal and one foul tooth to be pulled. I was still driving home, when the vet called me to explain that they detected FORL and will have to remove some more teeth, which includes removing some more money from my purse. I told them to do whatever is necessary and drove the last few kilometers back to my house. Monk and FORL. What a bummer!
Collected him in the afternoon. He was no longer drowsy, but very shy and went into the back garden immediately. I let him go - we have 26 degrees outside. No problem.
Monk will need antibiotics from tomorrow on, for five days. I have no idea how to master giving him a pill, but I will think something up. Firstly, Monk never cooperates (took me two attempts to get him into the carrier this morning!), secondly, I never ever had to give him anything. He was healthy all the time. Didn´t even catch a cold. And now this!
Bianca had asked me to bring the wild kitten to the vet for a general check-up, including parasites. All was fine and she was behaving nicely. There will be not much to tame - easy peasy. I did a giardia test on her after coming home. Negative. Named her Kalea, for the time being.

July 16, Friday
Things are not so well today. Kalea´s poo is too soft! And Monk is not eating at all. Just lying on the bed, not even drinking and usually, he is a very good drinker, compared to other cats. He must be in pain, but I can´t give him any pain killers, since he won´t eat anything.

So off I went with Monk to the vet again. She gave him several shots: antibiotics, pain killers and appetizer.
Let´s hope that it works.

July 18, Sunday
Kalea is doing well. Eating, playing and getting the odd cuddles from me and also my hubby. She likes that and purrs, but she is still a bit iffy with strange or loud sounds.
Monk is not doing well at all. Haven´t seen him eating over the last two days. He behaves normally, but wouldn´t go outside into the back garden, which is very unusual. I have an appointment for his shots anyway, tomorrow, so let´s see if they find something that is bugging him.

July 19, Monday
And yes, they found a lot. The vet examined Monk and found an infection around his gums. They kept him for checking his teeth again, and I told them to do an X-ray, since we are dealing with FORL. They knocked him out and I went home. This will take a while.
Got Monk back in the afternoon: X-ray showed more evil, as I had suspected. Three more teeth had to be pulled and some root canal work was also done. Poor Monk! I collected him around 4 p.m.
More shots will follow. Monk will keep me busy the whole week.

July 20, Tuesday
What a terrible day! Starts with Monk not eating still. Went on with Ursel telling me that Tetris escaped. Damn!

He was supposed to be released later in the afternoon. Ursel was really sorry and told me that it was hard to hold him anyway, since he wanted to leave so bad. It is the mating season, and hedgehogs can get pretty wild around this time. Still, I wish he would have stayed just a few hours longer, and we would have had a happy end. I hate explaining all this to the lovely woman, who found him and was so eager to get him back. I am heartbroken.

But the worst is, that the sister of my sister-in-law told me that the kitten had died this morning. He had developed some problems already yesterday, and she had taken him to a vet clinic. There, she was told that something was very wrong with his kidneys. I feel really sorry for the girl. She put so much effort in this. But to be honest, it was clear that the kitten´s chances were very slim. If you don´t have experience with rearing a kitten weighing around 200 grams or less, and - at the same time - don´t have a vet at your hand who gives you the necessary support, you are just doomed. And even if you have all this; it might still go wrong and you never know why. Nature is cruel.

I really don´t want any more bad news today. I am so tired.

Oh wow! Just when I thought, I sign off for now, something really fantastic happened:

I went out to feed my outdoor hogs a little late today, due to the stress. So I hurried through the front door around 11 p.m., when I heard a huffing noise in the shrubbery right next to the door. I couldn´t believe my eyes! There were Buddha and Ipanema sitting opposite to each other, Ipanema huffing loudly at Buddha, who was obviously courting her.

I was so thrilled, I nearly forgot to put the bowls down. Anyway, I hurried back in to get my camera and took some pics from a safe distance. Come on, Ipanema, let Buddha do what he has to do - we want some hoglets around here!

July 21, Wednesday
And off to the vet again with Monk. Another shot of antibiotics and something new: She gave me an ointment, that I am supposed to rub into Monk´s ear. It should make him eat, she said. Hmm. Well, I will try anything, that makes Monk eat again.
Saw that Monk was eating a little towards the evening, one hour after I rubbed the ointment into his right ear. So far, so good!

July 22, Thursday
Had to prepare and sign the documents for Phoebe. Yes, she is coming! My Phoebe from Minsk, Belarus. I had announced that I will be in Berlin over the weekend and asked, whether that would help, since the transporter doesn´t stop near Hamburg, and that was why Phoebe´s transport was delayed. But now, things are getting serious.
Had to say good-bye to Kalea today. Returned her to our cat shelter, since she needs company of her own age. In the shelter, Bianca had another kitten "on box" which was released into her kitchen today, after treatment, so we put Kalea down right next to him. They cautiously sniffed each other and then started playing together. That was so good to see. Kalea, dear girl, this is was you need and I wish you the best.

It was eerily silent in my living room this evening, and even my husband said that he missed her.

Monk was eating a little, but I am still not satisfied. Just a gut feeling. I had discussed this with Bianca also, earlier at the shelter, and she said that I should insist on subcut fluids. Otherwise, she said, he just might not get his strength back and will refuse food. Bianca´s experience is always worth a thought, so I will do as she said.

July 23, Friday
Insisted on the fluids when I was at the vet´s with Monk and they immediately concurred. That done, he got another round of antibiotics, and that should be it. His remaining teeth, gums and wounds look acceptable, and he should really be his old self again soon. Fingers crossed!

My hubby and I will be on our way to Berlin this evening. Partly due to some urgent private business, and Sunday, on our way back, we will collect Phoebe from Belarus. Let´s hope, all goes well.

July 25, Sunday
Collected Phoebe, who had arrived yesterday and stayed overnight with some animal friends, and drove home. Phoebe slept mostly through the voyage and once at home, I put her into my study and closed the door. But not before having left some food and water in there, plus setting up the camera.

July 26, Monday
Saw her using the toilet around 6:30 when I peeked through the cam via cellphone. Good girl!

Later, I went in to clean up and give her breakfast and fresh water. She had been eating during the night, obviously, but her poo is watery. Well, I have to collect some anyway for a giardia test. Only if negative, I will introduce her to my Bulgarians. Colour-wise, Phoebe reminds me very much of Trinity, an old cat I had, that had died last year, and that was a Tortoiseshell as well.

July 28, Wednesday
Had a home visit concerning a dog from a Bulgarian shelter. The family was awfully nice, and I will give a green light for sure. Already looking forward to the follow-up in autumn.
On my return, stopped at the cemetery to fill the water bowls.
Back home, did some work in my study, where Phoebe resides in her cat cave. Big step forward: while I was sitting at my desk, she ventured out of her cave, ate some cat biscuits, went to the toilet and even crossed the room to sit on a cardboard box, which is a lot closer to me than her cave. Wow! Do I see some trust building up already?

July 29, Thursday
Dropped some cat food at the lady, that looks after the stray cats in our village. Then drove over to Sabrina, who lives ten kilometers away and had adopted two cats a month ago from Spain. The home visit I did, on May 11th, if you remember. One of her cats has a massive infection, and we discussed what to do about it.

He is on antibiotics, but I have a feeling that the meds should be changed, since the situation has not at all improved. Sabrina will give me an update after her visit at the vet´s.

Phoebe: still the same. Sitting in her cat cave, sometimes venturing out and sitting on the cabinet across the room. I can´t touch her yet; she hisses at me. And I let Ramses in to sniff her. She hissed at him too. So far, so normal.

July 30, Friday

Had the trail cam out, hanging over the dry food station. Saw only one hog, which I couldn´t identify as one of mine, since there were no obvious markings. I wonder where all my regulars are. Well, since it is raining a lot these days and my shrubbery is lavish, they probably find enough insects to survive and can do without my hog restaurants for a while.

July 31, Saturday

Hung the cam over the wet food station for a change. Oho! So much hog activity during the night. Saw several hogs, some with markings, some without. Saw them running into the wet food station and also taking a sip from the shallow water bowl. They all look good: round-shaped, no apparent injuries, no tick infestation. Still, the time is nearing, when I will collect most of them for the annual check-up, including fresh markings and tick removal. Mind you, by collecting my hogs once a year, I collect important data concerning our ecosystem.

August 1, Sunday
The weather is still lousy. We are facing a lot of rain these days. At least, that´s good for all the animals, that usually suffer from dehydration during the summer months.
Went to a lady who regularly provides me with cardboard boxes for hedgehogs (sleeping quarters) and got three boxes. Drove on to Ursel, gave her one of the boxes (Ursel is in need of boxes all the time, due to the many hedgehogs she cares for) and discussed the latest developments. Hedgehog-wise, it is eerily quiet, even for Ursel, compared to last year. But her health situation worries me a lot: She is suffering from serious backache, plus a problem in her left hand. The hand will be operated towards the end of the month. Well, Ursel is, after all, 82 years old. Please God, give her some strength! I left the trail cam with her. We really hope to spot Tetris on it, if he is still around. Fingers crossed!

August 2, Monday
Sent *A game of spines* to Jenny. Since she is a hedgehog expert, I had asked her to have a look, check for mistakes and hopefully promote it among hedgehog friends. Besides, I spoke to Mrs. O., an old friend of Ursel, who lives in central Germany, and we discussed the current hedgehog situation, and how we can get a better and tighter network. Some rescues are filled up to the brim (especially where she lives) and some hardly get hedgehogs at all. This lady, 77 years of age, is, like Ursel, an experienced hedgehog rescuer, and it was a pleasure establishing contact to her. Mrs. O. was very friendly, and we will keep in touch.

She was thrilled when she heard, that I had produced a game about hedgehogs and ordered one immediately.

August 3, Tuesday
Fright in the night: Amira and Lucas, the adopters of Piccolo and Pepe, called me around 1 a.m. in the morning, totally upset. Something was very wrong with Piccolo! He wouldn´t eat, keeps hiding and is behaving oddly, they told me. While I was asking them questions (I suspected some poisoning from what they described), Piccolo threw up. That´s good, I said, so he is still able to get rid of whatever bugs him. I advised them to keep an eye on him over the next hour. If it is getting worse: take him to the emergency vet service. If he is getting better: go first thing in the morning.
We spoke again around 9:30. They said that he was slightly better, and that they had taken him to the vet´s who gave him some injections. If he is not getting better soon, I told them, they should insist on a blood sample. I still believe that he had gobbled down something wrong while being outside, but you never know. Better safe than sorry, right?
Bianca is coming back from her holiday in Bulgaria today.

August 4, Wednesday
I decided that it is time for the annual check-up of my outdoor hogs now. Around 10 p.m. (with dusk setting in) I started sneaking out to see who is munching at my feeding stations. Didn´t have to go far: Right at the water bowl, there was a hog sitting (and sipping) who had no marks. Ha! A new one! I took him in for a closer look: male, 950 grams, two ticks behind the right ear.

But apart from that he was looking good! I marked him with a "U" and let him go. Only took 10 minutes. Mind you, if you know what you do and what you are looking for, this quick pick-up is not stressful for the hogs. They forget it just about immediately. Have a happy life in my garden, Ustinov!

Went out four more times that night, but only saw Ustinov again, nibbling cat biscuits at the dry feeding station. I really hope to see some of my "old" hogs again soon.

August 5, Thursday

Got a call from a rescue nearby: Could I take over a hog in need, found around 30 kilometers away? Would be brought over later in the evening. Yes, of course.

Nothing wrong with the hedgehog, they said. Only a bit weak, they said. Looks good, they said. Well, all of a sudden they discovered flystrike and came a lot earlier than planned.

I was just back in the house, soaking wet from a thunderstorm that surprised me, when cycling back from the village six kilometers away, when the door rang.

To cut it short: Flystrike was an understatement. I would call it a nuclear invasion! I am not going into details, let me just say, that I was somehow through with the basic treatment around midnight. With one hasty dinner break. Ah, and another break for feeding the cats and the outdoor hedgehogs.

I have no idea what to expect next morning. I am completely exhausted. Named him Voltaire.

August 6, Friday
Well, Voltaire is still alive, but very weak and has lost weight over night. At least I couldn´t find fly eggs any more. And no maggots. Good! Gave him subcut fluids nearly every hour. The thing is, you can't just give the full amount to a weak hog, only little by little, over the time. Also gave him a shot of antibiotics. Plugged in the heating pad - but lowest degree!
If he is not picking up soon, I will have to carefully syringe-feed him towards the evening.
Shit, he wouldn´t eat. Neither by himself, nor by syringe-feeding. More subcut fluids. I am scared.

August 7, Saturday
Ran down to Voltaire first thing in the morning, expecting him to be dead. But he was still breathing. Lying on the side. I know what that means, and tears rolled down my cheeks. I felt so helpless. Discussed the situation with Ursel and two other hedgehogs experts (one was Jenny, and the other one was Nadja, who runs a professional hedgehog rescue station in Bavaria, together with her Mum). All three said: Let him go in peace!
I wrapped him in a soft towel and bawled my eyes out. Ursel had said, that this could take quite long. I checked on him every half an hour. Still breathing. Around half past three, I checked on him again and saw that there was white foam around his mouth, and he was breathing with his mouth open. I gently stroked his head and said good-bye. Then I went outside to mow the lawn. When I came back in around a quarter past four, he was dead.

Put him in my hedgehog box with coolers, so that I can bring him to the lab on Monday. I want to know what happened to him! We have a very high death rate this year in all hedgehog stations. And, as I mentioned before, there is a definite relation between the increasing death rate and our continuous destruction of nature. We need plants, weeds and natural, "untidy" gardens for the survival of insects and hence hedgehogs. Voltaire´s weight should have been around 1.400 grams instead of 700. What the flipping hell are we doing to our world?

I am so sad, so angry, so tired.

August 8, Sunday
Went about my daily work like a robot. And I look like some character out of "Resident Evil" too, with all the lack of sleep.
At least, Phoebe, who is with us now for two weeks, is giving up her shyness a little. She has moved from my study to my bedroom and has tried out all the cat beds available. This morning, she even came into my bed to say hello. She still sneezes a lot, so I will have to take her to the vet´s soon.
Ursel came over this afternoon, with my trail cam, for tea and cake. But right before Ursel, another hedgehog arrived: A female with 355 grams, very small and with maggots! Heike, the lady that found her, was awfully nice. Probably because she also does voluntary animal welfare work. It will be a pleasure to return Wolga (yes, that´s her name now) to Heike, when the treatment is over. But first things first. When Ursel arrived around ten minutes later, we had a closer look at Wolga.

Tiny maggots around her feet, and they had already started nibbling at them. Yuck! We killed the maggots and treated her feet. Poor thing. But this case is not hopeless. As I saw later, she is eating quite well.

August 9, Monday
Took Voltaire to the lab this morning. On my way back, I stopped at the cemetery to fill the water bowls. Made an appointment for Phoebe at the vet´s for Friday. Had another close look at Wolga: No more maggots. Treated her wounds. She has gained only six grams overnight, but so far, no worries. Hedgehogs are under stress the first night: new voices, new scents, new everything. I am quite sure that she will eat more tonight. Fingers crossed.

August 10, Tuesday
Shit! Wolga lost weight again and is at her starting point with 355 grams. Okay, I want to know what is bugging her and gave the poo sample to my local vet, for fast analysis.
Since I am away the next two days, I will leave Wolga with Ursel. Packed the girl, drove over and told Ursel about the latest developments. Ursel gave her an antibiotic shot, and then we waited for the vet to call. Aha, capillaria. Now we know what to do. See you in two days, Wolga.

August 12, Thursday
Collected Wolga from Ursel. She had gained weight a little (Wolga, not Ursel!). Good. That's the right direction.

Got a call from Amira: Piccolo is limping! I gave her some advice and tried to calm her down. Seems to be an ongoing story with Piccolo.

August 13, Friday

Phoebe has eaten next to nothing since yesterday. I only heard her drinking water at night. Went to the vet with her. Result: High fever, lung infection. She got all the necessary meds and we went home. Her weight was down at 2,3 kg. Not good. More prayers.

August 14, Saturday

Wolga has lost weight again. I will change her meds and think of a different menu for her.

At least, Phoebe has started eating a little. I am running a hospital, for all I know.

Amira called to tell me, that they found out that Piccolo had been bitten by the neighbour´s cat! He was treated and is better now. Thank God.

Had the trail cam out last night. Saw two hogs between 10 p.m. and 2 a.m. One of them was definitely Gandhi. Saw clearly the markings on his back. So glad, he is still coming over.

Went out around 10:40 p.m. to search for my hogs and found Gandhi! Took him in for check-up: 1.325 grams, no ticks, some fleas. He is looking good. Renewed his marking and let him go again.

Saw Ustinov too - at the dry food station.

August 15, Sunday

Wolga has gained weight! I am so relieved. But Phoebe is still not well. At least, she drinks a lot and eats a little from the small dry food pellets.

Checked the trail cam from last night: Saw Buddha and Gandhi.

Started the next round of telephone follow-ups for the animal shelter, that we are friends with. So far, all is well. Dogs and adopters: both happy.

Went out in the dark to collect more hogs for check-up and found Buddha! He was in good shape, had no ticks, one or two fleas and 1.076 grams. Fresh marking and off he went!

August 16, Monday
Wolga is still on the way up. Now at 391 grams. Good girl.

Went to the vet clinic with Phoebe to get a stronger antibiotic. And it worked nearly immediately. Back home, she started eating, drinking and roaming about the house. I can´t believe it.

When I thought that this was all for today, I was completely wrong! Around 5:30 p.m. the doorbell rang. There was a lady with seven hoglets standing in the door. The mother was, so she was told by the finders, presumely dead. Bitten by a dog. Took the bunch in and started feeding right away. Then called Ursel who came over around 9 p.m. She took over three of the babies, told me, that they were less than three weeks old, and off she went. Oh my God ...

August 17, Tuesday
I am dead tired. Took me a while to get back to (short) sleep after the night-feeding. Around 10 a.m., the doorbell rang. It was the same lady; in her hands a cardboard box. They might have found the mother, she said. Obviously not dead. If I could have a look.

Took the lady in and examined the hog. Yes, that´s a feeding Mom. Bingo! Put Mom down to the hoglets, who started twittering excitedly, and then Mom dragged them all into the sleeping box, one by one. It was so moving to see the reunion of the family. Called Ursel, since the remaining three hoglets will have to come back, now that Mom is taking over. Went to bed and slept for an hour. Drove over to Ursel and collected the hoglets, put them down to Mom and silently left the room. Before I went to bed, I checked on the family: They were all cuddled up together in the sleeping box. Good night, kindergarden!

August 18, Wednesday
Weighed all the hoglets, as Ursel had advised. This is important, because, unlikely as it may be, Mom might not accept all of them. Well, they all gained weight, but number six only three grams. That is not much. He was one of the three that came back from Ursel last night. I will check tomorrow again. If he is still dodgy, I will have to handrear him.
Wolga is at 420 grams now. Phoebe is eating again. Things are looking up.

August 19, Thursday
Mom is eating a lot. Good. All the dishes I put down for her are empty, whenever I check.
Went over to some friends to play *A game of spines*. They had played it with me already during the developing process They liked the finished version a lot and bought one. Cool.

In the evening, Annika, another animal lover (she is in the bird rescue scene), came over to have a chat and buy a game. I love Annika a lot and wish we could meet more often. At least, she lives in my village.

August 20, Friday
Went to the vet with Phoebe. They took a blood sample, a big one! Phoebe was not as stressed as I thought she would be. Thank God.
Weighed the hoglets: all gained, apart from number 2,3,5 and 6. When Mom retreated to her bedroom box, I got those four out, one by one, and syringe-fed them, to supplement.
Got Mom's poo sample result: Capillaria and a huge amount of lungworm. Will start treatment tonight. Mind you, with a feeding Mum, you have to be careful, concerning medication. Not everything is allowed. Same goes for pregnant hogs!
Posted a pic of Mom with her babies in the facebook group "Hedgehogs!" (which is an English group that I had joined originally to obtain hog vocabulary for this book, but stayed ever since, because I liked the group so much) and got over 1,600 likes for it! I have never ever got so many likes for anything I had posted in social media in my entire life. I was speechless. The nice comments also blew me away!

August 21, Saturday
Woke up with Phoebe lying in the cat bed next to my pillow. I was very moved. This is a great step forward for her, regarding trust.
When I checked on Mom and the babies (I call them the "Seven Up"), she was feeding them.

So the daily weighing procedure had to wait until evening. Syringe-fed three of them afterwards.

August 22, Sunday
Had the trail cam out. But on the footage, I only recognized Gandhi for sure. Still, there must have been a lot of hog activity during the night - all the feeding bowls were empty.
Don´t like the look of Phoebe. She only lies in my bed, not moving much. Hardly eating.

August 23, Monday
Asked my favorite vet (who is also treating our shelter cats) whether I could bring Phoebe in. My gut feeling says, that I shouldn´t wait any longer. And since I will drive up to the shelter anyway ...
So, got started early today: Dropped Phoebe at the vet, then went over to our cat shelter. Phoebe's examination will take quite long, including an X-ray of her lung.
Rang the vet when Bianca and I finished our shelter work. He will keep Phoebe over night, he said. She had developed a fever as well, he added. Later that night, I got the results from the extensive blood test that was taken on Friday at the other vet. FIV had been confirmed, but now it turned out that she might have FIP as well. Jesus!
Back home, went to the cemetery to fill up my water bowls. I was longing for some fresh air.

August 24, Tuesday
Talked to the vet: He will keep Phoebe another day, until all the results have come in.

At least, the fever decreased and she is eating again. But the situation is still critical.

Went over to Glückstadt (23 kms from my home) to have a look at Heike's garden, to see, if we can release Wolga here again. Beautiful. What a great area to release a hog. Wild overgrowth everywhere! Walked around and chatted for an hour in her garden, then returned home.

August 25, Wednesday
Drove up to my favorite vet to collect Phoebe. He said the fever is gone, and that she could go home, but when we opened the bandage where the vascular access had been, it started bleeding again! My vet didn´t like it, put the bandage back on and told me to wait for an hour. If the bleeding doesn´t stop, he wants me to come back. Since Bianca was expecting me in our shelter, I took Phoebe there, and we waited for an hour. Then carefully unwrapped the bandage again. Still blood coming. So I got her back to my vet. He injected something to drop her blood pressure and took a biopsy. I don´t want to go into detail, but there might be a lot more going on than just a heavy infection. Unfortunately, I didn´t understand everything my vet said. But I do remember destruction of red blood vessels, and that doesn´t sound too good to me.

August 26, Thursday
Glad to be home the whole day, since yesterday really killed me. Phoebe is hiding under a cabinet in my study. All the trust, that I tried to build up, vanished into thin air again, due to the constant vet visits. I am so sad!

What is more, she is not eating much, but has to: I am supposed to give her an antibiotic every day, together with her food. Please eat, little Phoebe, I am only trying to help you!

Got Mom from the Seven Up family out the first time since her arrival, to have a closer look at her, plus give her a shot against fluke. She looks okay. Exhausted, of course, but no ectoparasites or wounds.

August 27, Friday
The plate was empty. Phoebe ate during the night, oh good! The others are doing well too: Wolga is at 526 grams today, and the Seven Up are all gaining weight and starting to steal Mom´s food from the plate. They are so lovely to watch.

August 28, Saturday
Went over to Ursel with all seven babies. Mom stayed back home and had a chance to relax for a while. We split the babies among the three of us: No 4, 6 and 7 went over to Gudrun, another fosterer in our vicinity. No 1 and 5 stayed with Ursel, and No 2 and 3 (the weakest ones) will go back with me to re-unite with her Mom. We gave them all a shot against fluke (very important, even or especially at that age!), had some tea and cake. Then I said my good-byes.

August 29, Sunday
Wow: all of them gained weight. Number 2 and 3 and even their Mom. I named her Xena, by the way. Number 2 (the male) is now Yoda and number 3 (the female) now Zoey.

God, I am glad that those awful last three letters are over! Next hedgehog's name will start with A again.
Phoebe is also eating well. So is Wolga. Today: only good news!

August 31, Tuesday
Went to my favorite vet with Phoebe. He took another blood sample, to compare the results. "We have no indication for FIP", he told me. He explained the medical treatment (one pill, every three days) and, of course, examined her. Phoebe had gained weight and was a lot fitter. My vet hopes that she will still have plenty of months, but can´t guarantee it. With FIV you just don´t know.
Went over to Bianca to tell her everything. And I took "Big Noodle" home with me. Her kittens had already been adopted, and Bianca thinks that Noodle might fit in well with my cats, so therefore she is coming along today. We will see how it goes.
After having dropped off both Phoebe and Big Noodle, I collected Wolga (593 grams today) and went over to Glückstadt. Heike was waiting there for me, and we released Wolga in this wonderful garden. Have a happy life, Wolga, good-bye.

September 1, Wednesday
Warmer weather again. Filled the water bowls at our local cemetery.
Big Noodle is doing okay. She was quite lively and noisy during the night, but that is pretty normal after a move. They either hide or they are restless. I heard her meowing nearly non-stop all night. Yawn!

September 2, Thursday
Big Noodle is chilling on the window sill most of the day. In the evening, she wants to play, and I toss several balls around. She loves chasing things.

Got a call from a lady (Jenny B.), that found a small hedgehog, diurnal. She brought him over and I examined it. Male, 386 grams, some ticks. Welcome aboard, Anatol.

Talked to the manager of the garden colony, where I had released Wolga. She is very enthusiastic about my idea to give a speech about hedgehogs at that colony. We hope to find a date for the end of this year or next spring. All depends on the bloody pandemic ...

September 3, Friday
Phoebe is not eating obviously. Hmm, I've got to observe this (again).

Got a call from one of my vets: Whether I could take over two hoglets from Wacken: small wounds (presumely dog bite), flystrike, diurnal. Okay.

They arrived an hour later. Chapeau to the vet: He managed to remove all the fly eggs; I couldn't find any. They also gave them an antibiotic shot. Good. Most work done. I gave them something against maggots and fly eggs that we might have overlooked, just to be on the safe side. Weighed them. Both below 150 grams. That will be tricky.

Big day for hog mom Xena: Released her in the evening at the place where she was found. Let her go with 1,150 grams. That is perfectly okay, especially since this is a terrific natural area, plus, food and water will be provided.

Big Noodle has settled in, I would say. But, due to her young age, she wants to play nearly all the time. I try to keep her busy as much as I can.

September 4, Saturday
Phoebe is still not eating. I agreed with Bianca that, if she won´t eat the following night, I will bring her to my favorite vet tomorrow. In case you wonder: Yes, my vet also works on Sunday, and Bianca works there on Sundays too. So, I will set up the trail cam, this time indoors, to find out whether Phoebe is eating or not.
Filled water bowls at our neighbouring cemetery on my way back from Ursel. Ursel also has hoglets, but they are only around 50-60 grams. Ursel believes that one won´t make it. We had a quick cup of tea and chat together, then we had to split again. Those are busy times, when you are in the "hog business".
Oh no! Found out that one of the Wacken-brothers lost body temperature and weight. Quickly prepared a hot water bottle for him to rest on. Changed that twice. In other words: went to bed around 1 o´clock, hoping that I was not too late. Prayers.

September 5, Sunday
Was prepared to find that hoglet dead in his hoggy sleeping bag. But no! He was warm and moving. Thank the maker! And, after having fed him with warm rearing milk and, of course, having fed all the other animals here in my private zoo, watched the footage from the trail cam, that recorded the cat feeding place over night: Ramses, Ramses, again Ramses, Monk, Big Noodle and ... Phoebe! Good! That means, she is eating after all.

Maybe she is still stressed by the whole situation and just wants to eat in peace. Full of hope now, I gave her a bowl with the pill that she has to take every three days. And yes, she ate that too.

One of the mornings, when I could hug the whole world!

September 7, Tuesday

Extremely busy days. Where do I start? Phoebe: seems to eat. And is moving a little around the house. So far so good.

The hoglets: Well, we are not out of the woods yet. Zoey had been the weakest from the start, and she is still very weak. Actually, she is losing weight again, so I discussed it with Ursel, and we agreed that she will need some antibiotics. Ursel, who got number 1 and number 5 from the "Seven Up", also complains that number 1 is not gaining. I will send in another poo sample. Sometimes, the first sample does not show all the parasites involved. When in doubt, a repetition is never wrong.

The Wacken-brothers from Friday are also tricky. One (named him Bacchus) is very weak and not gaining. The other (Caesar) is doing fine. I collect their poo too.

What is this, with one out of two creating problems? I keep checking, feeding, weighing all day. But mainly, I am worried about Zoey. She is so thin, and I need to know what is going on. And fast!

September 8, Wednesday

Went over to our cat shelter. Did the invoices with Bianca, looked at the new entries.

One of them is a poor sight: Male kitten with traumatic brain injury and paralysis in the hind legs. Probably car accident. Then stopped at Andi to give him his first edition of *A game of spines*. He was very moved. Finally seeing the result of work that lasted several months is always a very magic moment.

Quickly went home to feed Zoey and Bacchus. Zoey is still difficult to feed, but Bacchus is eating well and started eating by himself while sitting on my lap. Is that the big turnaround for him? Half an hour later, he was dead. I am at a loss for words.

September 9, Thursday
Went to the vet with Zoey, Caesar and the dead Bacchus. Even the vet has no idea what had killed him. We gave Zoey and Caesar the necessary shots and discussed how their treatment should continue. Zoey is still losing weight. It is so annoying. She just wouldn´t eat without help. I have to feed her at least five times a day. Her brother Yoda has twice the weight she has by now! Discussed it with Ursel as well. We are running out of ideas.

Phoebe was downstairs and even came near me. I gave her some treats and she ate them. I still can´t touch her, but this is a huge progress!

September 10, Friday
Zoey is still losing weight. I will give her another antibiotic, and then I have done everything I could. Suddenly the big surprise: She was eating without my help for the first time! In German, we say "Hope dies last". Well, words to live by.

Anatol is close to 500 grams now. He will be released next week. To get used to the temperatures, I put him into the enclosure on my patio. More room and interesting scents for him to pick up.

Bianca came over for a quick visit, on her way back home from Hamburg. We talked about the two young cats, that I will foster for some days, arriving on Sunday from a household, that was completely overstrained with them. They will come all the way over from Wismar, which is at least a 90-minute car drive to my humble home. Besides, Bianca took Big Noodle with her, since she is not really happy here. Noodle is, after all, a very playful cat, and my cats are not playing at all. Well, Monk sometimes, but he prefers sitting in the backyard observing the mole. It was worth a try, but Bianca has already found some nice adopters for her, so it is better for Noodle to go there, before she is bored to death here with my weird cats.

September 11, Saturday
Hooray!!! Zoey gained 20 grams over night. Just unbelievable! The antibiotic seems to be working.

Sabrina had called me a few days ago. Amelio, the cat that had the bad infection, hasn't recovered yet, and no vet she went to, had been able to do something about it. Plenty of antibiotics had been shot into the poor cat to no avail. Sabrina had been so desperate when we talked, that I had sent her to my favorite vet. She went there today, and my vet did a thorough check-up, with the result that Amelio got his infection due to a bad tooth! That tooth will have to be removed soon.

Sabrina thanked me over and over again for having sent her to my vet, since she had spent so much money on vets for nothing (plus the fact, that the cat was still having problems). Glad that I could help.

September 12, Sunday
Zoey and Caesar: gaining weight. Anatol and Yoda: losing weight. More medication.
The cats from Wismar arrived around 2 p.m. The family (father, mother, daughter) were in bits and pieces, crying a lot. I nearly started crying myself. I know how hard it is to give away your animals. But sometimes you have to. For the well-being of your pets. I am sure we find them a lovely home very soon – the two cats are very cute.

September 13, Monday
Got a call from a lady that found a hoglet in her garden. Went over to check it: Sound and healthy with perfect balling-up reflex. I told her to feed it, release around dusk, and watch if it is going back into the large log pile where I suspect its Mum and the nest. Hoglets are a tricky thing: If we rear them (especially when they are very small), they might die, since the rearing milk is never as good as the milk they get from their Mum. I told her to give me updates on the hoglet and watch out for others in the vicinity. If they appear to be alone, I will return immediately and take over.

September 14, Tuesday
The Wismar-cats are doing fine. And all my four hoglets have gained weight over night. Thank goodness.

Tonight, I returned Anatol to the place where he was found. But: I wanted Jenny B. to keep him in an enclosure for some days before she releases him. And I told her to add some special powder to the food in order to restore his intestinal flora. She will inform me daily on his weight, and then I will tell her when his time has come.

September 15, Wednesday
Brought Caesar, Yoda and Zoey over to Heike, the nice lady that had found Wolga. She will feed them while I am away (another funeral - will this ever end?). They will have their own room in the garden shed. I trust Heike completely. She has both the experience and the commitment.

September 20, Monday
Collected my three hogs. They all gained more weight and looked good. Heike did a brilliant job!
The Wismar-cats must have missed me a lot. They went bananas when I came into their room. Hey guys, I was only away for three days! Besides, I have a fantastic catsitter, whenever we are away. Nevertheless, that was really cute to see, and I must admit, I missed them too.

September 21, Tuesday
Had the cam out last night: Saw Gandhi (several times), I think Buddha (once) and an unmarked hedgehog (twice). My wet food station was busy from 8:50 p.m to 5:30 a.m. Empty bowls in the morning. I reckon the hedgies are filling up their tummies for the big sleep.
Took Phoebe to the vet, to check on her weight. Oh wow, she gained some. She is at 2.57 kg already.

That really thrilled me. A month ago, I was not sure whether she will live to see the next month and now this! I owe this all to my favorite vet. He is *the* Sherlock Holmes concerning animal deseases, if you know what I mean.

September 22, Wednesday
That was a loooooong and busy day. Packed the two Wismar-cats and went over to Sabrina to collect her cat Amelio. First stop was Andi's house: I dropped him some of the hedgehog board games to sell. Then, went to my favorite vet to drop Amelio there. He will be operated on his tooth tomorrow. Sabrina has to attend professional school this week and couldn´t bring him in. But she will collect him tomorrow. Then I went over to Bianca to drop the Wismar-cats. They will move into their new home soon, but I had a hard time leaving them behind. They had been unusually affectionate, especially the male. Sniff.
Before going home, I refilled the water bowls at one of my cemeteries. Back home, fed all animals, weighed my hogs and gave them their meds. And then, after dinner, I went out to check on my outside hogs. Found Ebo at 8:15 p.m. and brought him in for a check-up. One tick (on the belly), some fleas, but apart from that, looking good. Gave him a fresh marking and let him go.
An hour later I saw Gandhi, but I didn´t collect him, since I already had him in some weeks ago. Gandhi is still fat. A bit later, I found Ipanema at the dry food station and took her in. No ticks, some fleas and with a bit more weight compared to last year. Ipanema is the hog that Buddha was wooing during summer.

I wonder whether he was successful and she has had babies. So far, I haven´t seen any.

September 24, Friday
Took Caesar and Zoey to Brigitte, a friend of Ursel's, who also fosters hogs now and again. Caesar and Zoey will be on "holiday" here, since I will be away for around ten days, and they are not ready for release yet.
Checked on my outdoor hogs at night. Three times in total. Saw Ebo (twice) and Gandhi (once). No sight of Buddha or the others. I hope to see Buddha again before he goes into hibernation. For no specific reason. Just because he is my favorite outdoor hog.

September 25, Saturday
Big day for Yoda. Released him where the "Seven Up" and Xena, their Mum, were found: In our neighbouring village. Yoda says good-bye with 674 grams.

October 7, Thursday
Have just returned from my holiday yesterday, and hogs are already queueing up at my door! Took in two today: Dali with 251 grams and some internal parasites, but nothing serious. And Elrond, with 258 grams. He might be tricky. I saw a sort of swollen front leg (which is bad news) and he loses spines.

October 9, Saturday
Dali and Elrond are eating well and gaining weight. Good! Picked up Caesar (933 grams now!) and Zoey (569 grams now!) from Brigitte, who did a terrific job.

I will put Caesar into the enclosure on my patio, so that he can get used to the dropping temperatures. He has enough weight for release.

My regular outdoor hedgehogs seem to prepare for hibernation already: The food bowls were still full this morning - for the first time!

Got a call from Heike around 8:30 p.m. A friend of her had found a hedgehog with 80 grams. No time to lose! They brought him over around 9 p.m. Put the hog on the scales: 71 grams. But teeth all grown. That means he is very poorly indeed! Put it on heat and fed it later. Thank God, it is eating. But I will check on it during the night.

October 10, Sunday

Fed the hog again around 4 p.m. So far, so good. Or so I thought. In the evening, it stopped eating. Oh, now what? Will it die during the night?

By the way, Cole had to be put to sleep today. Cole of "Cole & Marmalade", the famous internet cats. That really broke my heart. I have been a fan of them and Chris Poole´s work for more than eight years. I can´t believe that Cole is no longer with us.

October 11, Monday

But the hedgehog is still with us. Don´t know how it managed to stay alive. But still not eating. More subcut fluids.

Went to our cat shelter around noon. Bianca asked me to take over three kittens, since she already has plenty to deal with. I took them home and started bottle-feeding immediately.

Now the house is really full: my three cats, the three kittens, Caesar, Zoey, Dali, Elrond and the new hog, which I named Flora. What a zoo!

October 12, Tuesday
Flora had died during the night. Another battle lost.
Took Elrond to the vet to check on his front leg. Nothing wrong with it. Big relief! Both Elrond and Dali are eating well and gaining weight.
Moved Zoey to the patio enclosure, so that she can adapt to outdoor temperatures.
Released Caesar in Heike´s paradise garden. Good luck, little man!
Went to Ramona in our neighbouring village to check on four hogs. She had taken them in while I was away, and I had guided her through the fostering by telephone from Istanbul and Rome. The hogs looked good, and I administered the required shots against fluke. Now waiting for poo sample results.
Chapeau to Ramona – the hogs are in best hands here.

October 13, Wednesday
Named the kittens "The After Eight", since they came in very late for the time of the year. They are gaining very slowly. I wish I could get them to eat some baby food. They have already got all their teeth, so I hope we go into second gear any time soon. Since one is female and two are male, I named her "The Girl". Her two black brothers look nearly identical, but one of them has a bit of white fluff behind his right ear. So I named him "White Ear" and the other one "No Ear", for the time being.
Buried Flora today. With a flower, as usual.

Poo analysis from Elrond showed no endoparasites. Wow. That´s a nice change.

Released Zoey in the evening. After Xena and Yoda, she is the last one to return to her homeland. The other hoglets from the "Seven Up", that stayed with Ursel and her friend, will be released somewhere else. It would be too much to release eight hogs in the same garden. Hogs are loners by nature, after all.

October 14, Thursday
Oh my God, what a day. The kittens are not eating properly, and it is really messy feeding them by trying to feed them with the spoon (and later the plate), in order to get them used to kitten food. Went over to Ursel´s to have tea, cake and a chat. While I was there, her phone rang and someone needed help with a poorly hog. Ursel was just about to say that she was full, when I whispered that I still have capacity. Thirty minutes after I arrived back home, a lady was at the door with a hog full of flystrike! It was massive. All over his poor body! Started treatment immediately, but was interrupted by another caller whom Ursel had directed over to me. They had a cold hedgehog to offer. And again: started treatment immediately. In other words: heat! But not literally. You have to warm a cold hog very very slowly!

I am not sure which one will make it, or if they both make it or none of them. No idea. I am just exhausted.

But the names are set: Gimli for the flystrike guy and Hafiza for the ice-cold lady.

October 15, Friday
Found Hafiza dead in her enclosure. It was just too late.

At least, Gimli is still alive, but not eating by himself. So I fed him. Then, had a closer look at him, in case I overlooked some fly eggs, but couldn't find any. Seems, I did a thorough job last night. Tiredly, patted myself on the shoulder. Gimli is a sweet boy, and I hope he will make it.

Still spoon-feeding the kittens. Oh please, why don´t they eat by themselves? That would save me so much time. Sigh!

Deathday of Nike. A year ago, when I was just bringing more food to my foster hog Paddle-Bianca in my study around 9:30 p.m., Nike was lying dead on the ground. She had heart issues and left us at the age of 15.

October 16, Saturday

Deathday of Titus. A year ago, around 9:00 in the morning, I was doing the dishes in the kitchen when Titus suddenly started throwing up. Then, both his hind legs gave way, and he was dragging himself along the floor, screaming. I rushed him to the vet immediately, who could only save him by putting him down. Titus also had a terrible heart desease. And my guess is, that he was so upset about Nike´s death the night before, that he had a stroke.

Yes, that´s right. Last year, I lost both Nike and Titus within twelve hours. And I still can´t believe it.

Back to the present and the kittens: No Ear is eating without my help. Oh good! Gimli is also eating alone. That is brilliant news!

October 17, Sunday

Gimli is gaining weight. So are Dali and Elrond. But the kittens are not. Something must be very wrong with them, but I cannot grasp it. Talked to Bianca on the phone for a long time. She said, her kittens in the shelter are the same. Not really gaining, some with giardia (I tested mine: test was negative), and most of them had been in a terrible state from day one, when they were brought in. So, what can we do? Bianca will send me some tablets. She hopes, that they do the trick.

October 18, Monday

The Girl is not well! I can tell from her movements. Yesterday, she was running about, alive and kicking and today, she is just sitting in a corner. Besides, she has thrown up and suffers from terrible diarrhoea. That´s it: appointment at the vet´s! And again, none of them have gained weight. Had a poo sample ready to come along. Vet said, could be Calici or Parvovirus. All three of them got a shot for their immune system. Now waiting for result of poo sample.

Returned home around 8 p.m. An hour later, a couple was standing in the door with two hedgehogs. Obviously Mum and child. Both massively infested with fleas! I looked at Mum´s eyes and saw that she was packing for the rainbow bridge. A bit of infusion and warmth, then cuddled her up in a blanket and put her in a stressfree and dark zone. She will die within the next two hours for sure. As for the child: mild treatment for the fleas, then food and water and put it into a prepared enclosure. Its tummy is warm, that´s a good sign.

103

October 19, Tuesday
Isra (Arabic for night journey) had died over night as expected. But the rest of the zoo is doing quite okay: The kittens had eaten all their food and were loudly demanding more! Isra's baby, a female that I named Jamaica, had eaten her food also. Gimli, Elrond and Dali are doing fine anyway.
Put the three kittens on the scales: The Girl and White Ear have gained, but No Ear has lost a bit. Besides, he had started showing the same symptoms like the Girl: Throwing up and diarrhoea. Nice one. This is a never ending story, obviously. Bianca is still riding the Parvovirus theory, but I am not yet convinced.

October 20, Wednesday
Had the After Eight at the vet's again. They got another round of immune booster, and No Ear got an extra shot of cortisone. Still waiting for the lab results concerning the poo.
My four hogs are all doing fine. Thank heavens!
Got a nasty call from a lady, that had captured a hog two days ago, which was entangled in a net in her garden. I told her to see a vet first and let him decide whether the hog needs help or not. If the hog is okay, she could just feed it until hibernation and it won't occupy space in my house. What makes finders keep an animial for so long, not knowing what to do? And when the damage is done, they bring the hogs over, so that people like me can bury them. Sometimes this is very frustrating. She didn't even know what to feed. Would *you* keep an animal in your house, that you know nothing about, without seeking professional help?

October 21, Thursday
Got a call from a lady my age that had a hedgehog for some time with lungworm. She was desparate for medication and advice and glad, she found me. Since she is quite fit with hedgehogs, and her hog has no other problems and gaining nicely, I will supervise from a distance, whenever she needs help. That call was so different to the call last night. She was really enthusiastic about nursing hedgehogs and eager to avoid any possible mistake. Now that's the spirit, we fosterers like.

Had a video chat with staff members from both *Four Paws* and *Tierart* (the latter is a wild animal shelter in South Germany, under the wing of the global organisation *Four Paws*) about the wildlife card game, which will be about the animals, that you can find at *Tierart*. As the game designer, Andi was attending too. Next step will be my visit at *Tierart*, getting to know the staff and the animals in order to go into detail with concept and design. That will be fun, and I am really looking forward to that.

October 22, Friday
The After Eight is doing well and gaining weight. Same goes for Dali, Elrond, Gimli and Jamaica. They all look good. Got a new entry today: Kalea, 214 grams, some fleas. Weak. I will do my best - as usual.

October 26, Tuesday
Didn't find the time to write earlier, with lots of things happening here.
The After Eight kittens' situation has improved a lot, and they will return to our cat shelter on Friday.

Kalea, the new entry lost weight over two days, and I was really worried. But, after another medical treatment, she gained weight again, scales showing 241 grams today. But she is certainly not out of the woods yet! Dali and Elrond moved into the enclosures on my patio for temperature adaption. They will hopefully be released on Friday evening. They have gained enough and are ready for hibernation.

Gimli and Jamaica are also gaining. They are still together in one enclosure, since, at that age, they need some snuggle company. Weight-wise, Jamaica has passed Gimli today. Chapeau!

I have applied for another cat from Varna, Bulgaria. That cat, Pixi by name (I will change that to Phoenix, should the adoption be confirmed) has a crippled front leg and is extremely shy. Well, so is Phoebe. Maybe such a cat is good for my Phoebe-girl – or so I hope.

October 27, Wednesday
Kalea has gained weight. No Ear and White Ear as well, but the Girl has lost a little. And her poo is a bit dodgy again. Hmm. That called for another round of deworming medication.

A young lady from my neighbouring village appeared with a hog, that she had in care for already a month. Lolita (that's her name now) is suddenly losing spines, and the lady wanted me to have a look. I put my gloves on, since I suspected ringworm. And right I was.

October 28, Thursday
All kittens have gained weight. But Kalea has lost some grams. Now what?

I still have her under treatment for bowel infection, but without the poo sample result, I don't know what is bugging her. Hopefully, it won't come too late.
Lolita's weight has increased a little.

October 29, Friday
Bianca's husband collected the After Eight around noon. Good bye, kittens, have a happy life!
Ursel came over for tea and cake and had a look at Lolita. She gave me some useful advice for her treatment.
Took Dali and Elrond to their release area in the early evening. Dali had around 700 and Elrond was well above 650 grams. They are more than ready for their deserved freedom. And they are the last hogs, that I dare to release this year. From now on: Definitely supervised hibernation on my patio, since night temperatures will be mostly below eight degrees soon. Only minutes after I had put down their boxes in this kind lady's garden, Dali peeked out, sniffed the air thoroughly and started a wild self-anointing party. That is always so cute to watch!

October 30, Saturday
Went over to Amira and Lucas, the adopters of Piccolo and Pepe, with a cake. We had a nice chat and tea together. Piccolo and Pepe recognized me both and let me cuddle them. They are so great together, and Pepe is a lot bigger now than last time, when I saw him. Piccolo was even sitting with us at the dining table. Piccolo is still the boss, Amira said. I guess, that will never change and why should it? Pepe is very happy with his role as the younger brother.

October 31, Sunday
Collected the second hog, that was in care at the lady, that had brought Lolita. She suspects that this hog has ringworm too! Anyway, it needs professional care now, so she was glad that I took it in. Another female! Named her Moldau. Okay, now I have Gimli, Jamaica, Kalea, Lolita and Moldau. Five out of ten possible places occupied. Nine is my personal maximum, concerning the overwintering period, and one box remains empty for emergencies. Well, the now empty boxes will be occupied in no time. All hedgehog stations are already full to the brim!

November 1, Monday
Phoebe has thrown up! That's very bad, since it means the effect of the pill, she has to take, is gone. I hope that it's nothing serious.
Having spoken of empty boxes: Got another hedgehog from our neighbouring village: 213 grams, female. Named her Niobe. I will have a closer look at her tomorrow.

November 2, Tuesday
Went over to Ramona who was still fostering those hedgehogs, that I am supervising from a distance. They were gaining weight too slowly, so I recommended a change in the food supply. Besides, I want her to add some oil to the food. Their skin is a bit dodgy, and I think one of them has started to lose spines.
Put my own hedgehogs on the scale: All gained, only Kalea has lost a little.

Poo sample had shown a lungworm burden, which I was treating, but now I will have to change her medication, since the current meds had no effect until today.

Had to treat Lolita's ringworm by carefully picking the infected skin. Lolita really hates that, but it had to be done. Poor thing. Her ringworm is really massive. The rest of the hogs are doing fine, including Niobe. Had checked her thoroughly. Nothing to worry about. Besides, she has a healthy appetite.

November 3, Wednesday
Phoebe has thrown up again. Now I am really worried.
Went to our cat shelter around noon. Did invoices and stuff and had a chat with Bianca: We are trying to get our disabled cat Lucy to a cat shelter in Graz, Austria, that specialises in disabled cats. Lucy was found some weeks ago and brought to our shelter. We had hoped, that the paralysis in her hind legs might only be temporary, but we had to bury that hope after the last check-up. So far, we have no idea how to transport Lucy to Austria, but need to find a solution until the end of November. She can't stay in our shelter forever, since she needs special care.
Bianca called to say that she got another kitten in a very bad state. What the hell is going on this year?

November 4, Thursday
Phoebe seems to be better today. Phew!
Put my hedgehogs on the scales: all gained weight, only Kalea lost again. I think she is dying. I gave her every treatment I could think of – my heart is bleeding.

Heike came over with her hedgehog Micha. Gave a shot against fluke and checked her through. Looking good and gaining weight. We had a quick chat and a cake, before Heike left again.

Bianca called to tell me that the kitten has just died. "I am so sick of all these avoidable deaths", she said with an exhausted voice. I wish I could give Bianca a firm hug.

11:30 p.m.: Checked on all hogs before going to bed. Found Kalea dead in her sleeping quarters. My heart still breaks every time I lose a battle, but at least she died warm and cosy and not out in the cold, alone. Rest in peace, tiny Kalea. I will miss you. Called Bianca to tell her that she is not alone facing just another death. Both Bianca and myself will have a hard time to find sleep tonight.

November 5, Friday

Jenny B. (finder of Anatol) came over with another hedgehog, called Bosse. He revealed 400 grams on the scales, and, after the check-up, I gave him a shot against fluke and handed Jenny B. some meds for capillaria, as detected in poo sample, that she must give him over the next seven or eight days.

November 6, Saturday

After having played *A game of spines* with a family with many kids (who bought three games, one for themselves and two for friends), I stopped at Ursel's, to discuss our medication supply. I will organize some necessary meds next week.

November 7, Sunday

All my hedgehogs have gained weight. Started lungworm treatment for Lolita and Moldau today. I will split the medication and give it over two days instead of one, since they are still young, and I don't want to trigger any bad side effects.

Started collecting poo from Niobe and Gimli/Jamaica. Yes, Gimli and Jamaica are still together in one enclosure. I was meant to split them up long ago, but they love each other so much! They have separate bedrooms but sleep in the same one every single night! And there is no huffing or fighting. Ursel said, I could keep them together under these circumstances, but will have to split them up, when they awake from hibernation at the latest.

By the way: I think, Gimli is the one that has to do the household. Usually, after I have cleaned up their two bedrooms, I see them disappear in one together. Then, I rip some newspaper pages (for them to build the new nest) and put it in front of their houses. Soon after, Jamaica sends Gimli out to collect the paper. That is so cute!

November 8, Monday

Lolita is my main problem. The ringworm is still massive, though I treat it everyday. She gets her regular medicated bath, and I remove as much of the bad tissue as I can. But Lolita hates the whole procedure, jumps up and down, hisses and tries to bite me (with success, once). We still have a long way ahead of us. Sigh!

November 9, Tuesday
Went over to Ramona to give her some meds for her hedgehogs. I am supervising the hogs of three ladies now: Ramona with hers, Heike with Micha and Jenny B. with Bosse. Just imagine, I had those hogs also here in my house. There would be no more room for emergency cases. I am glad, that the girls are so dedicated to our prickly friends.

My hogs are doing well. Gaining weight, getting their necessary treatments. Only Lolita … well, I think I got the ringworm myself now. Have found some weird red dots on my hands. Well, that's not the first tiime, and I know how to treat myself. No worries.

You see, with a jumpy hog like Lolita, you can wear all the gloves you want. The spines will go through. And so does the ringworm.

November 11, Thursday
Another case of "Why?": A lady contacted me some days ago about a hedgehog she was nursing. She is completely unexperienced and, instead of bringing the hog over immediately (as I told her), she waited, went to the wrong vet, and – as expected and seen many times before – the hog died last night.

Why can't folks listen to what we fosterers say? A diurnal hedgehog needs help. Almost always. Another life gone. For what? The lady is shocked. I am frustrated. End of story.

November 12, Friday
Went to the vet to get some meds for my hogs and stopped by at Ursel's to give her some as well.

Got the result of the poo samples from Gimli and Jamaica: Fluke! Treated them right away.

November 14, Sunday
All my hedgehogs are gaining weight, but Lolita still looks awful! I believe that there is an underlying mite problem, which should be treated simultaneously. And so I did. Let's see, if that does the trick.

November 15, Monday
Oh! I have a feeling that the treatment worked already. Lolita is looking a bit better this morning.
We finally have found a way to get our disabled cat Lucy to Austria. But that includes me, hitting the road in two days! Okay, here I am, rushing to organize all the necessary tickets and a hotel, since I will make a detour, before returning home.

November 17, Wednesday
All my hogs gained weight. But I am still not satisfied with Lolita's ringworm. Since I will be on a big tour from tonight on, I left Lolita with Ursel. She will take care of her while I am away.
Bianca and her hubby collected me around 7 p.m. to take me (and Lucy) to Hamburg's main train station. I will go to Rosenheim, which is in the very South of Germany, where I will meet Andrea, a cat lover from Munich, who will pick up Lucy next morning and bring her to Graz, Austria. Our Lucy will finally go to her new home: The shelter for disabled cats, that I mentioned and that I had visited twice over the last three years. You find a chapter about that shelter in my book *Pfotenengel*.

I had booked a private compartment for Lucy and myself, so that I could let her out for a while. She lay with me on the bed, and we were listening to a podcast. I had to change her incontinence sheets twice, but Lucy didn't mind at all and slept mostly through the whole adventure. She is such an adorable cat.

Late at night, my father messaged me: Kismet, our family stray cat at the Black Sea, is in for surgery tomorrow. My dad had found her thin and in no good condition and had taken her to the vet. Obviously, she had a big wound, and now we are both worried, since there is a risk that she might die during surgery or due to the anesthetic.

November 18, Thursday
Around 8:30 a.m. I handed Lucy over to Andrea, who will drive her across the border to Graz. Lucy arrived at her new home at noon. A lot earlier than me, by the way. I continued my journey in direction to Pirmasens, since I will visit *Tierart* tomorrow.

My dad messaged me with an update on Kismet: The surgery went well and she is back home. My dad will spoil her rotten now. God, I am so glad. My Kismet is a very special cat, and honestly, I could write a book just on the adventures we had with Kismet over the last ten years!

November 19, Friday
Visited *Tierart* and had a look around. Many tigers, foxes, racoons and even a cougar! Well, the tigers are still my favorites. Ever since I visited *Felida* in Holland, I am addicted to tigers.

After the tour, we discussed the concept of the card game, and around noon, I packed my bag and got ready for the long way home.

November 20, Saturday
Knackered as I was, I went over to Ursel to collect my Lolita. She looked good (ringworm-wise), but hadn't gained weight at all. Ursel suspects more lungworm and she is probably right. I will have to treat her for lungworm again. At least, all my other hedgehogs had gained weight nicely. Gimli, the only male in my foster care, came close to 700 grams. So out he went: into one of the enclosures on my secured patio. He is the first hog to be out, and I hope that he will hibernate soon. I guess that the next one will be Jamaica. It should have been Moldau (with 650 grams), but to my utter disgust, I discovered that she is losing spines. Now what? More ringworm? Oh, please!

November 22, Monday
Collected a hog from the far North of our country, in the evening. Poo sample had shown zillions of lungworm, so I started treatment right away. Ophelia, that's what I named her, has 500 grams, good shape and had been fostered by her finders so far. But I decided to take over, since her treatment is not so easy, and her weight has not improved over the last days. You just never know: The heavy lungworm infestation might have started to cause lung problems. I better have a close look.

November 23, Tuesday
Ophelia has not eaten at all over night. Well, as I mentioned before, this can happen, when a hedgehog is unsettled by the move. Let's see, how she is doing next night. Put her on the scales. She lost 15 grams.
Moldau has lost weight too. That is strange, since she was the one with the best appetite.

November 24, Wednesday
Ophelia has not eaten at all. I need special meds from Ursel, so I called her several times, but no answer so far. This is serious, and I am running out of time!
Moldau the same: weight loss. Gave her a shot against fluke. She had one already, some time ago. But her poo sample had shown a huge amount of fluke, so nothing wrong with treating her again. Here is one lesson on hedgehogs: Never underestimate fluke!
Speaking of problems: I try to keep Ophelia alive with subcut fluids, until I get Ursel on the phone. Where is she, for Christ's sake?
The other hogs are doing okay. I think, I will move Jamaica onto the patio in two days. She has the perfect weight for hibernation. And she is fit as a fiddle.

November 25, Thursday
I am very worried about Ophelia. She had eaten a little, but that is far from satisfying. At last, I got a hold of Ursel to get some advice. She told me to give her an antibiotic shot, going along with the lungworm treatment. And she recommended syringe-feeding. Okay! Well, not okay, since Ophelia wouldn't let me syringe-feed her. At least the antibiotic shot was done. More prayers needed. It would be awful to lose her!

November 26, Friday
All hogs gained weight, but Ophelia didn't. However, she had not lost any and was obviously rummaging around in her enclosure during the night. I even found some poo. Still, the situation is tense, and she is far from safe!
Jamaica has reached her weight for moving out onto the patio. Gimli, who is out for some days now, is still not at all thinking about hibernation, it seems. His enclosure is a mess – every day!
Saw some strange stains on Moldau's nose. Whatever it is, it sits very firm and is hard to remove. Asked Ursel what to do. She will come over on Monday. Good. Since Moldau also loses some spines, I have a suspicion what I am up against.

November 29, Monday
Ophelia is at 530 grams. This is like Christmas and Easter on the same day to me! Good good girl, I am so proud of you! Gimli and Jamaica are still awake in their outdoor enclosures: empty food bowls every morning.
Ursel was here in the afternoon and had a close look at Moldau and Lolita. First Lolita: Ursel thinks she is doing fine. Ringworm gone. The spines will grow back. Nothing to worry about. Then Moldau: Ursel frowned when she examined her. "You know what that is", she asked me, pointing to the stains on Moldau's nose. "Mange, right?" Ursel nodded. Well then, that's easy to treat. Just wanted to make sure, that I was not mistaken.

November 30, Tuesday
Went over to Ramona to have a look at the hogs she fosters.

They have moved to the outdoor enclosure, but are still awake, just like mine. Gave her some advice, had a coffee and a chat and off I went. Next was a call from Heike – about her hog Micha. Treatment for capillaria is done. Micha has been gaining weight and is now well above 650 grams. She can also move into the outdoor enclosure, I told Heike.

December 2, Thursday
Took over an old cat that will spend her last days in my house. Named her Smilla. She is quite weak, due to bad and insufficient treatment in her previous home. I hope that I can give her some last good moments before she will pass.
Jenny B. called to tell me, that she found another hog. Bosse, the hog she cared for, had moved outside (supervised hibernation), so now she started looking after Cindy, who has 400 grams. She will collect the poo, and once we know what we are up against, I will come over with meds. Anatol, Bosse, Cindy. Jenny B. picked up my system with the alphabetical naming, I realized with a broad grin.

December 3, Friday
Smilla had eaten overnight. I have made her a cat bed right next to the radiator, so that she can enjoy the heat. And she loves it, obviously. She also purrs loudly whenever me or my hubby bend down to cuddle her. I doubt that she can walk far, let alone jump. But for now, she seems quite happy, with cat bed, toilet, heat, food and water.

Maren, the finder of my hog Gimli, came over and gave me the money they had collected for me, when she threw a charity party for Gimli and my hedgehog fostering last Saturday. It was overwhelming to see that there are still people caring about what I do. We had a tea and a chat, and I promised to keep them updated on Gimli.

Got another hog in the evening from Christine, who lives about ten kilometers away from me. The hog is underweight (355 grams), but otherwise okay: no injuries or ectoparasites.

December 4, Saturday
Pushkin, the new hog, had eaten well. Put all my hogs onto the scales. They are gaining in small steps, so I am still waiting for the next candidate for my outdoor enclosures. My guess is, that it will be Niobe. She is around 600 grams now. I give her another 2-3 days.

December 5, Sunday
Pushkin is at 400 grams. Gave him a shot for fluke.
Ophelia is at 581 grams today. There is some magic going on, for sure. Around ten days ago, I thought that she was dying. You just never know with hedgehogs.
Smilla: She comes out, the minute I approach her, eats, then returns to the cat toilet to lie there. Hmm, what does that mean?
Got a call from Jenny B.: Cindy is not doing well. I told her to come over tomorrow, if Cindy won't eat overnight. We must get the fluke under control, before we start anything else. As you can see, I am leading anything but a boring life.

Speaking of which: Another hog arrived in the afternoon: abscess, underweight and some dodgy pus on the cheeks. Since I am currently too busy, I passed him on to Ursel in the evening, who will take care of him.

December 6, Monday
Jenny B. came over with Cindy. She was at 443 grams. Gave her a shot against fluke and gave Jenny meds for possible bowel infection. We will be waiting for the poo analysis.
Went over to Ursel in the afternoon: Ursel updated me on "Flo". That's the hog from yesterday. The abscess still needs intensive care, and Ursel also started antibiotics. Mind you, they are a must, when treating an abscess. Flo is a seasoned hog with only 996 grams, meaning, he is way too thin. Poor Ursel got herself quite a challenge.

December 7, Tuesday
Gimli is asleep! I couldn't believe my eyes when I went outside. His enclosure is tidy, food and water untouched. With some hope, I turned over to Jamaica's residence, but fat chance: She had been partying as usual. But with temperatures close to zero, she'll be asleep pretty soon. Niobe has not passed the 600 line yet, so I will wait three more days and check again.

December 9, Thursday
Smilla was not herself this morning: ignored the food and just sat in the cat toilet, not moving, not purring, not getting out when I approached her. Saw some saliva coming from her snout. Tooth problem, I bet!

Took her to my local vet in the afternoon. Returned with Smilla, pain killers, antibiotics and meds for her ears. She has a tooth problem alright, but also an ear infection.

December 10, Friday
Smilla is her old self again! She eats well and purrs loudly whenever I go near her. I am relieved.
Niobe has moved onto the patio today. With 625 grams she has bought her ticket to hibernation. She will get the room on top of Gimli. In a few days, Ophelia and Moldau will follow. Lolita is still more than 100 grams away from outside, and so is Pushkin.
Got another hog this evening, 327 grams. Not eating.

December 12, Sunday
Sunday, lazy Sunday …. not!
Phoebe has severe breathing problems and is sneezing since yesterday. And this morning, I saw that Smilla had stopped eating again. And the new hog, named Querido, has lost weight and is down to miserable 305 grams, despite all the meds I put into him. Called my vet, described the situation and asked him if I could drive up with some of my animals and who should be first in row, for today (emergency service, since it's Sunday!). His short answer was: "Pack all three and hit the road!" Any questions, why he is my favorite vet? I guess not.
Packed Smilla, Phoebe and Querido and drove up. Smilla: her bad state has obviously to do with her hyperthyroidism! When Smilla had first shown up at his vet practice, my vet had told Bianca and me about the surgery, Smilla will have to undergo soon.

Seems that we have reached this point now. Poor thing. I will leave her with Bianca for three days, since my vet wants to check Smilla tomorrow again.

Phoebe: another viral infection. She got some shots and will also be back on Wednesday for check-up.

Querido: My vet immediately analysed the poo sample that I had carried along and spoke of tons of capillaria. Well then, we know the enemy now, can fight it and hopefully, we are not too late. He gave Querido some subcut fluids and an appetizer-shot. I took Smilla over to Bianca's house and returned home. Hurried outside to feed my patio hogs. Then the indoor hogs with meds and everything. Then the cats.

I am completely knackered. Sunday, lazy Sunday ...

December 13, Monday
Moved Moldau out onto the patio, with 725 grams. She took the last apartment in the winter skyscraper. Moldau is on the ground floor, Gimli on the first and Niobe on the second floor. Jamaica has a detached enclosure for herself.

That makes four out of eight, that are outside now.

December 14, Tuesday
Querido is finally eating! Not much, but enough to have some hope again. I am still syringe-feeding him the meds he needs. Without those meds, he would be dead by now.

December 15, Wednesday
Drove up to my favorite vet with Phoebe. She is still not well, but her breathing improved a bit.

He gave her another round of shots and told me to give antibiotics again in two days.

Collected Smilla from Bianca. Had a chat, then drove back home.

My hogs: all gaining, even Querido. He is at 335 grams now. Better than before, but still far away from good.

December 17, Friday

Hooray! Querido has 370 grams. I am thrilled. The only way is up, from now on!

Andi, my graphic designer was here, and we discussed the development of the wildlife card game. We have to have it ready before Easter. Fingers crossed.

Took Phoebe to the vet again, in the evening. She got another antibiotic shot and will need another one on Monday.

December 18, Saturday

Jenny B. called me yesterday night to tell me, that she found another hog. She brought it over today: It's a female, thin, 341 grams, but otherwise okay.

December 19, Sunday

All my hogs have gained weight. The new one, Riga is her name, has gained 30 grams over night. Must have been hungry. Outside, on my patio, the opposite: Not one hog had eaten. All fast asleep. Nothing to clean up. Octavia, who had 640 grams today, has moved onto the patio as well. That makes four remaining hogs: Lolita, who is growing her spines back, Pushkin, the easy hog, Querido, who has passed the 400 grams and newbie Riga. I guess that at least Lolita and Pushkin will move outside before the year is over.

December 20, Monday
Got Smilla over to my favorite vet: She will undergo surgery on her thyroid tomorrow morning. I am extremely worried, to say the least. An old lady like her, not eating properly, hardly being able to walk ... and a surgery like that. Doesn't make me feel comfortable at all.
Phoebe was also with me for another antibiotic shot. Let's hope that she is done with her infection for now. But with her FIV background, very unlikely. I have a close eye on her.

December 21, Tuesday
We have temperatures below zero now. Niobe, Gimli, Moldau, Jamaica, Ophelia: all fast asleep outside. As for the indoor hogs: all gained weight.
Smilla: surgery done. She survived, but looks awful.

December 23, Thursday
Smilla is purring a lot, but not eating. I tried to tempt her with various things, but to no avail. This is really making me nervous, I must admit. The other cats and hogs: all doing fine. Riga's poo sample has shown a mild infestation with capillaria. No sweat.

December 25, Saturday
Enough is enough. Smilla wouldn't eat, and I kept her going with syringe-feeding, hoping that she would overcome the effects of her surgery. Today, I drove up to my favorite vet, and he gave her subcut fluids and some stabilizing shots. I asked him, what he thinks what makes Smilla neither eat nor drink, and he reckoned that this has still to do with her surgery.

"I have never seen a tumor this big, and I have seen a lot!", he told me. Once again, Bianca will take over for the next three days, since Smilla needs more treatment. I will see her on Tuesday, when she'll get her stitches removed. On my return home, somebody called about a hedgehog that was roaming in their garden. I gave the first-aid advice and hope they pick the poor creature up, before it is too late. We have minus seven degrees right now. Hedgehogs should be fast asleep and not running about. This is serious!

Later in the night, Bianca sent me a video with Smilla drinking and eating. God, I am so relieved!

Merry Christmas – at last.

December 26, Sunday

Moved Pushkin (652 grams) out onto the patio. Hope, he will sleep just as tight as all the others there.

Bianca sent a message late at night: Smilla's situation has worsened. She was talking about kidney failure. My heart sank. And my fear rose, that I won't see her again.

December 27, Monday

Moved Lolita out onto the patio. She goes with a weight of 615 grams, and I wish she had a bit more, but she became so restless, that I believe she wanted to tell me, that the time for her long sleep has finally come. That makes seven outside and two inside: Querido and Riga will be staying for another couple of days, since they haven't reached their hibernation weight yet.

Haven't heard anything about the roaming hedgehog again. That is so sad. It will surely die, if they don't find it. With every single day passing, its chances of survival drop considerably. Not good at all.

December 28, Tuesday
Took Phoebe to my favorite vet. She had caught another infection, and my vet gave her an antibiotic shot. Then it was Smilla's turn: Bianca had brought her in, and the three of us discussed her situation. My vet thinks that there is some kidney failure going on, but not as bad as he initially thought, after having looked at her blood sample. Still, she was and is very dehydrated, and it will be tricky to make her drink more.
Got a call from Jenny B. concerning Cindy's poo sample: fluke (which I had treated already) and some mild infestation of coccidia. That can wait until she comes out of hibernation, I told her, since Cindy gained weight properly and is ready for her long sleep. We do poo samples of *all* hogs again anyway, once they awake in spring. That is very important: hedgehogs in care should be released squeaky clean – always!

December 29, Wednesday
Phoebe seems okay, but Smilla doesn't. She eats very little, and I have a hard time to persuade her to drink anything. She is apathetic again, just sitting in her cat bed, not using the toilet, not looking up, hardly moving at all. I know that I will have to let her go soon, but it hurts every time. Cried a lot during the night.

December 30, Thursday
Went to one of my local vets with Phoebe and Smilla. Phoebe for her antibiotic shot and Smilla for subcut fluids and stitch removal. When the vets came out and handed back both cats (we are not allowed in, due to Covid-19), they told me, that they wouldn't remove Smilla's stitches. They would rather put her down.

A wave of panic came over me, though I knew, of course, that this could happen. I took a deep breath and told them, that this was a decision that three people would have to make: my favorite vet, Bianca and myself. I called Bianca (who thankfully was on duty today) and passed on the shocking news. We agreed that I should drive up immediately.

So there I was: Driving up to my favorite vet again, with Smilla (and Phoebe, who was still around, of course), not losing any time. Arrived there at 7 p.m., totally exhausted – emotionally and physically – and waited for my turn. "No", said my vet, examining Smilla, "we still have a small chance. Her condition might have something to do with a substantial lack of calcium". He took some blood and removed her stitches. I wanted to know whether Smilla is in pain, though I knew the answer already. My vet would never try something to avoid euthanasia, if the animal is in pain. He just shook his head and said, that, if the blood sample proves him wrong, and if there is nothing else that we could do, we could still put her down then. Since Smilla will need subcut fluids again, I will have to leave her with Bianca once more. I shed a lot of tears during that examination and was holding Bianca by her arm for support. I have been in this animal welfare business for nearly twelve years now, but situations like these still touch me. Around 8:30 p.m. I drove back home with Phoebe. It was dark, windy, foggy and rainy, and the drive was terrible, but my thoughts were only with Smilla. Will I see her again?

December 31, Friday
My diary ends today. But some of the stories didn't end yet. You might want to know, what became of my hogs and of course Smilla, and since I still have to proofread the whole thing (again and again), it will take until the middle of January, before I will hand this over for print-out. So there will be a short update, before I leave you to it. As for today, I can tell you that Bianca sent me some videos with Smilla eating heartily, which really thrilled me. But the question is: Will she continue eating without the fluids that she still gets almost daily? Querido and Riga are gaining weight nicely. Querido is well over 650 grams and could move onto the patio any minute now. But I will have to wait some days for the weather to get colder again. We have around thirteen degrees now, and nearly all my patio hogs have awakened. Only Moldau is oblivious to the weather – good girl! As for Riga, she is close to 500 grams and, if she keeps the speed, she will move out in about 8-10 days too. Then all my hogs will be outside. But it won't take long, until the next hogs will move in: with underweight, badly wounded or severely dehydrated.

With the new year knocking at the door, I start to wonder: What will become of Smilla? How many hedgehogs will I be able to save in 2022? Will the cat from Bulgaria arrive in January, as planned? How will she fit in? And when will I be able to touch and cuddle Phoebe for the first time?

If you want to follow my animal welfare life in future, I recommend my instagram account, where I upload hogs and cats and the stories behind them. Maybe see you there one day. @bali_kiknadze

Wishing you a successful 2022, wherever you are. And be nice to this planet. There is no other. God bless.

Bali.

The promised Update

January 4: Querido moved onto the patio with 720 g.

Smilla, who was doing quite well for some time, had an awful seizure on the day, when I was meant to take her back home. She never recovered from that, so we had to put her down on January 12. Smilla was a true fighter, and Bianca and I are glad, that we were able to make her comfortable for the last days.

Riga, my last indoor hog, will move onto the patio around January 20.

The arrival of the Bulgarian cat is scheduled for January 30.

Paddle-Bianca, before release

Jade, after her bath

Flora, R.I.P.

the "Seven Up" family

me, feeding one of the hoglets

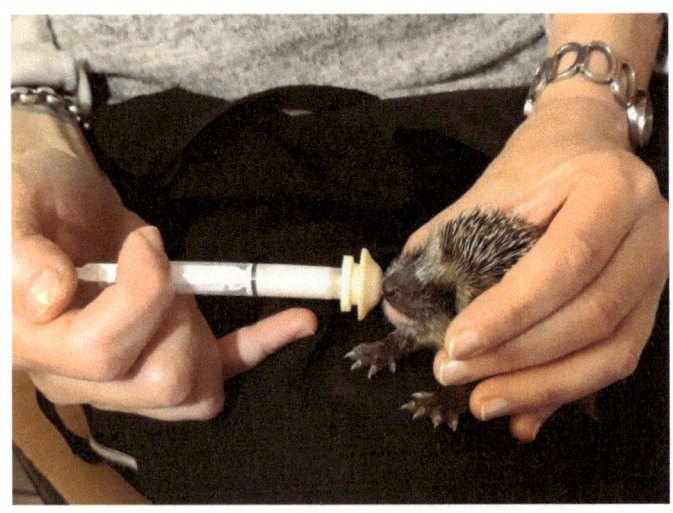

me, with Lucy, in the train

Monk and Ramses

the "After Eight" kittens

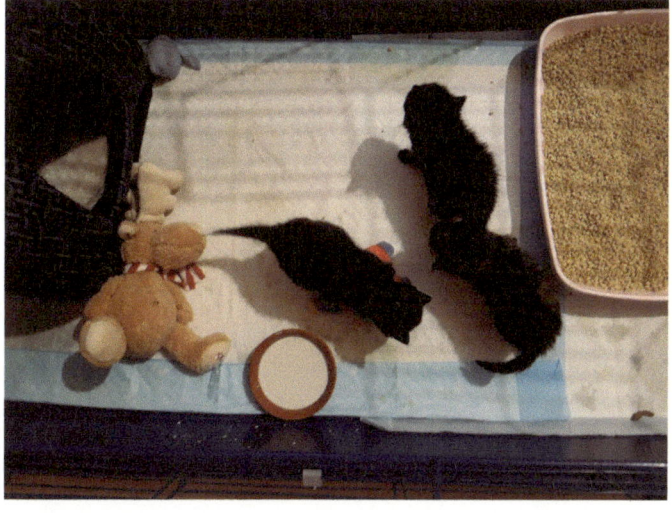

the winter skyscraper on my patio

Phoebe

Quincy, with massive flystrike

Tetris and his huge abscess

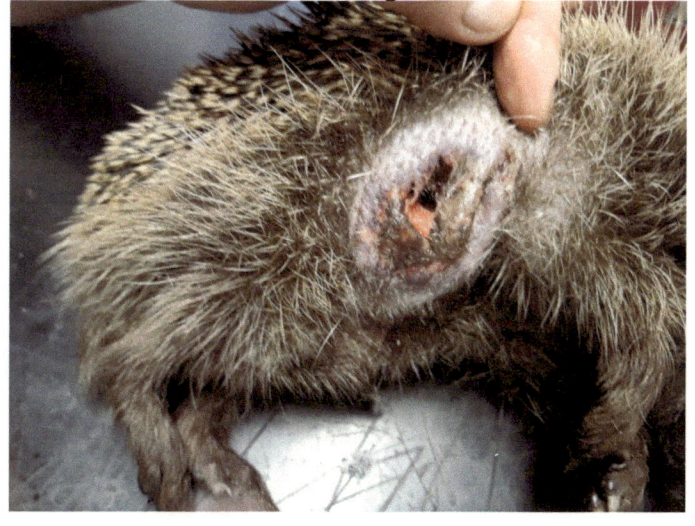

Gimli and Jamaica

Riga, waiting for hibernation

A big shout of praise to:

Theresa, Ina, Amy, Ian and Danielle for the nice drawings.
Jenny (Hedgehog Emergency Network)
Bianca (Stubentiger Eiderstedt)
My favorite vet, for being the best vet under the sun.
Ursel, my invincible hedgehog teacher
Andi, my graphic designer
Jenny, Heike and Ramona for taking care of hogs under my
supervision. I am sooo proud of you girls!
Nadja from Igelstation Otzing and Steffi from Igelhilfe
Schöffengrund-Weilmünster for your advice.
All finders that dropped hedgehogs in need at my place and
left some motivation, good vibes and/or money.
All the lovely girls working for the hedgehog emergency
network and all the hedgehog rescues that I am and will be
in touch with.
Facebook group "Hedgehogs!" for unvoluntarily supplying
me with the necessary hedgehog vocabulary and for your
nice comments, whenever I posted something in the group.
And for your incredible English humour!
Chris and Jess from "Cole & Marmalade" for raising
awareness, to say the least!
Everybody who cares for stray animals, TNRs them, feeds
them and does anything to improve their miserable lives.
Everybody who also cares about our wildlife.
All of you that work on a voluntary basis to help people,
animals or nature. You! Are! Awesome!
And last but certainly not least:
Everybody, who understands that the climate change is a
serious threat to our descendants and wants to be part of the
solution NOW!

You people are my hope. Thanks and hugs!

About the author

Bali Kiknadze was born in 1969 in Hamburg to a German mother and a Georgian father. She has lived in Germany, Turkey and in Ireland. Originally a marketing consultant and language teacher, she is now working as a book author and game designer, living with her husband and several cats in Northern Germany.

Books by Bali Kiknadze

Balistan
Pfotenengel
Wie tickst du?
Tagebuch eines Tierschützers

Outtakes

or

Stories that didn't make it into the book, but I wanted to tell you nevertheless.

Do you know how Pepe got his name?
When he was still a tiny kitten, we had a hard time finding out whether he was male or female. He was so fluffy on his belly, that we mistook him for female, for quite some time. His penis was covered in fluff! So, after finding out and just for fun, my hubby called him "furry penis", in German: pelziger Penis. And the abbreviation is .... Pepe!

Do you know that there is a bit more behind my alphabetical hedgehog naming?
It is also a secret tribute to countries, cities, people, you name it. The next hog's name will start with an S, so, if male, it will be Seamus. If female, I will call her Siobhan. That's the greeting to my friends in Eire, where I had studied and worked for a while.

There are some exceptions though. For instance, I have never played Tetris in my entire life!